Freedom Behind Bars
(Keys To Unlock What's Holding You Back)

By
Tom Naemi With Vanessa Denha Garmo

ACKNOWLEDGMENTS

I want to thank all the people who helped me on this journey that led to publishing this book. First, I want to thank God Almighty for His strength and His truth, for shining the light on the darkness in my life.

I want to thank everyone in prison ministry who led me back to Christ and helped me out of my prison cell.

I want to thank Bishop Francis Kalabat for allowing us to evangelize the faith as laypeople.

I want to thank everyone who volunteered their time in service for our prayer ministry and those who helped financially promote the healing ministry.

I enjoyed working with Vanessa Denha Garmo, who helped get my story on paper. I want to thank everyone at the Eastern Catholic Re-evangelization Center (ECRC) for their support of our healing ministry and for allowing me to share my story.

I want to thank our editor Jennifer Stang for her attention to detail. I want to thank Gail Coniglio for her publishing expertise. I also want to thank Dr. Cheryl Grigorian for her encouragement and support. Thanks to team who built the website and designed the book and cover. To all the family members and friends who proofread chapters, brainstormed ideas and gave us some needed feedback.

I want to thank you, the reader, for taking time out to read this book and think about how you, too, can break free from the shackles of sin and vices and find true freedom in Christ.

COPYRIGHT@2022

All Rights Reserved. No part of this book may be used or reproduced in any manner without permission of the authors except in the case of brief quotations in critical articles or reviews

ISBN: 978-1-958399-13-2
Imprints: Creative Book Writers

Designed by Branded Web Studios

Scripture texts used are taken from *New American Bible and The Great Adventure Bible* by Ascension Press.

For information about this book, please visit https://jesuslightofli-feministries.net/

DEDICATION

I dedicate this book to all those who participate in prison ministry. This is for the laypeople, evangelists, pastors, priests, and other religious people including religious sisters—all those who visit men and women in prison and pray for them and with them and share the Good News. It is through prayer and finding Christ that we find our freedom.

A NOTE FROM THE AUTHORS

This book is told from the perspective of Tom Naemi, who shares his testimony which includes his experiences and people he met before he went to prison and while in prison. Most of the names have been changed to protect the identity of certain people with whom Tom has since made amends. This is his testimony told from his voice.

DISCLAIMER

This book is for adult audiences. Tom Naemi spent nearly 16 years in prison; in this book, he shares some descriptive and disturbing experiences. Although relevant for these teachable moments, they may not be appropriate for all audiences and including younger audiences.

FOREWORD

I stood by a car at a park in West Bloomfield, Michigan, listening to this short-statured, bald guy talk about Jesus. In his street slang and boisterous voice, he talked about the three dimensions of faith. He recited scripture as if it were infused in him. I had just met him a few days earlier, but I had already heard about him.

When he was done talking, I walked up to him and was reintroduced to him by mutual friends. We became fast friends. My friends and I invited him to participate in our Eastern Catholic Evangelization Center (ECRC) Ministry, where he first started with a Bible study and then joined me in healing mass. I knew he had a gift from the Holy Spirit to lay hands on people and pray for healing.

He knows scripture fairly well. He has no formal education but is well-versed and knows how to share the truth. Jesus didn't reach out to the scholars to follow him. He reached out to fishermen and the tax collector. God uses men of our time too. "God uses the fools of the world to shame the wise. He uses the weak of the world to shame the strong. God uses the lowly and despised of the world, those who count for nothing, to reduce to nothing those who are something" (1 Corinthians 1:27-29). God, too, uses Tom.

In this book, Tom candidly shared his testimony to bring others to Christ. He lived in darkness for years until he found the light of Jesus by reading scripture and eventually surrendering his life to God. He continues to use his gifts to evangelize the faith and bring others to the Lord.

Tom was physically locked behind bars, but in reality, he was locked inside his vices long before he was sent to prison. He was locked in anger, rage, and fear, among other things. His testimony is an important one to share because he is not alone. Few may end up in prison because of anger and rage, but many are locked in all kinds of prisons; through his story and by the Grace of God, they too can find freedom by surrendering their life to Christ.

His message is an important one because it is truly through Christ that we live free in the world.

+ Francis

Bishop of the Chaldean Catholic Eparchy of Saint Thomas the Apostle in Detroit

Table of Contents

Introduction *11*

Chapter 1, "LOCKED IN ANGER"
Finding Freedom in the Virtue of Prudence *16*

Chapter 2, "LOCKED IN HATE"
Finding Freedom in the Virtue of Love *35*

Chapter 3, "LOCKED IN FEAR"
Finding Freedom in the Virtue of Faith *60*

Chapter 4, "LOCKED IN LIES"
Finding Freedom in the Virtue of Truth *74*

Chapter 5, "LOCKED IN DESPERATION"
Finding Freedom in the Virtue of Hope *87*

Chapter 6, "LOCKED IN RESENTMENT"
Finding Freedom in the Virtue of Fortitude *104*

Chapter 7, "LOCKED IN REVENGE"
Finding Freedom in the Virtue of Forgiveness *129*

Chapter 8, "LOCKED IN ADDICTION"
Finding Freedom in the Virtue of Temperance *163*

Chapter 9, "FINALLY, FREE" 210

Chapter 10, "YOUR INDIVIDUAL CELL" 225

Chapter 11, "HEALED TO TELL" 232

INTRODUCTION

"I will give you the keys of the kingdom of heaven and whatever you bind on earth shall have been bound in heaven, and whatever you loose on earth shall have been loosed in heaven" Matthew 16:19

±

One of my favorite paintings is *Christ at Heart's Door* by Warner Sallman—you know, the one where Jesus stands knocking at the door. The door has no doorknob. He stands there waiting for someone to open it. He doesn't force Himself in. No, the Lord patiently waits for you to let Him in.

You have heard many people say the phrase, "I have been to hell and back." We almost dismiss it because it has become a cliché, but then we hear the story. If I didn't change my ways, I was on a path to living eternal life in the fiery pits among the demons.

I was binding on earth evil until I was sent to hell on earth—to the U.S. prison system. It was there I opened the door where Christ stood knocking.

I was born and raised Catholic, and it is not like I didn't know God existed. I went to church. I was married by a priest, had my kids baptized, and I, in every sense of the word, was Catholic. In reality, I couldn't have been farther from God.

God calls us to love; well, I did that. Sure, I loved my life when I was successful. I loved my family and children. I loved my friends and had their backs just as much as they had mine. I missed the point, though. I hated my enemies. I hated my business competitors, and I was going to make them suffer.

I wanted happiness, but I created chaos all around me, and I put my family through it with me. I can't tell you in words how grateful I am for the nearly 16 years I spent behind bars, but I share with you my story because it was there, that I found freedom—and I found it in Christ.

You may be walking around this earth free from the shackles of prison, but you are imprisoned in yourself; you are locked up in addiction, in fear, in hate, in despair, in anger, in lust, and lies.

There is only one way out; the doors are unlocked, and He is waiting patiently for you to open them. I know my story sounds off the wall and not believable. I get it. Even people who were part of it might deny it because the truth is too hard or embarrassing for them to accept. I changed many names in this testimony you are about to read to protect the privacy of others, but it doesn't change the truth.

This is my story. This is my conversion. I say conversion, even though I was always Catholic. It was only by name. This is my journey. I share it with you in the hopes that maybe my hell can lead others to heaven. I want the whole world to know Jesus because Jesus wants to save souls.

This may read as an indictment of the prison system. I am not trying to take anyone on. I am merely telling you my story as I lived it. I found freedom in using the gifts I was blessed with to bring healing to others and to bring them to Christ.

One of the best years of my life was 2015. I sold my business after 10 years of working full-time in my ministry. I ended the year broke but the happiest I had ever been in my life. I was reminded that joy is found in Christ and in nothing else the world has to offer. Through this testimony, I hope you, too, will find joy in Christ.

— **Tom Naemi**

"Trust in the LORD with all your heart, and do not lean on your own understanding. In all your ways acknowledge him, and he will make straight your paths" Proverbs 3:5-6.

One of my favorite prayers is the Serenity Prayer: May God grant me the serenity to accept the things I cannot change, the courage to change the things I can, and the wisdom to know the difference.

However, surrendering has been one of the toughest things for me to do in life - to truly surrender to the Will of God. I, like many people, want to control every aspect of my life and every outcome. There are many aspects of Tom's life, and this story that intrigued me and prompted me to first write a cover story about his experience in the Chaldean News, a monthly ethnic magazine I co-founded and co-owned for nearly 16 years.

I knew then the story needed to be a book. As I wrote this with Tom, I envisioned scenes of his life like in a movie on the big screen. I also agreed to write this story with him because of his work in prison ministry. I see this book as a tool to reach people in prison and on parole. I wrote this with him to read like a movie unfolding, a story being told. One thing about Tom's testimony that struck me when I first heard it and stays with me today is when he sat on the bed inside his prison cell, acknowledging he made a mess of his life, and from that moment on, he gave his life to Christ —he truly surrendered.

I believe the first step of being released from the bondage of sin is surrendering. There are so many people locked in their own prison cells, locked in fear, anger, resentment, hate, and so many other things. I became passionate about Tom's ministry to heal people, to reach people in prison and to help them find freedom in Christ. This process has been a journey for me and has strengthened my faith along the way.

I often recite a surrender to the Lord's prayer when I find myself anxious about things in the world or when I am discerning major decisions in life, calling on the Holy Spirit to guide me. I hope this book encourages the readers to put their trust in the Lord.

— **Vanessa Denha Garmo**

Chapter 1

LOCKED IN ANGER

Finding Freedom in the Virtue of Prudence

"A fool always loses his temper, but a wise man holds it back"
-Proverbs 29:11.

±

"If they curse you, you curse them back," my dad said. "If you come home beaten up by one of them, I will beat you up again."

I really didn't understand the depth of that statement at the time, but years later, I realized it was my dad's way of teaching me to be a fighter and survivor. He knew how tough the world could be, even if he didn't know I would end up living thousands of miles away in a land called America.

It was 1959. I ran into our yellow brick house in Baghdad, Iraq, and jumped on my dad's lap. We lived near the market area, not far from the government offices. I was about 5 years old at the time and was often reminded that we, as Christians, were not liked by many people in our country.

We had eight bedrooms and fruit trees in the front yard, which was surrounded by an iron gate. The hallways were massive—at least,

LOCKED IN ANGER

that is how I remember it. We lived a lot better than most Chaldeans in Baghdad at the time. My cousins used to say we were rich compared to others. I don't really know. I was a kid. We went to Catholic schools. My mother actually had a washer and dryer, which was unusual for the people living in Iraq at the time. It was the kind of dryer with rollers that you fed the clothes through. We had a 24-inch television, and it was a big deal.

I had a couple of brothers who owned a bakery shop and another brother with an electrical shop, and my dad worked at Casino Baghdad. It was more like a nightclub and restaurant, not a gambling casino you'd see in the United States. It was for men only. He worked for my uncle, who trusted my dad to run the business.

Christians in Iraq have been the minority for many years, even though we are the original inhabitants of the land. Not only do we represent a small number of the population that has decreased drastically over the years, but we also have been persecuted for centuries. It's the reason we have been called the Church of the Martyrs. It is believed that no other Christian group has been killed in the name of Jesus and our faith more so than the Christians from Iraq.

There was a lot of prejudice, but not all hated us. The non-Christian kids were raised to hate us, even though we sometimes played with them. We were kids, after all. Kids in Iraq didn't have a childhood you would see in America. We didn't have Toys R Us.

When I was 9 and 10 years old, I worked at my brother's bakery in Baghdad during the summer. My brother paid me 50 cents a day. It was a lot of money back then. I worked at the bakery for months to buy myself a soccer ball. It was one of the few toys we ever had. All of the neighborhood kids came out to play with it. We didn't have music lessons or after-school activities. Buying a soccer ball was the talk of the town. We played soccer as much as we could, for hours and hours in the yard.

FREEDOM BEHIND BARS

I was about 10 years old around the time I could sense the roar of a lion growing inside of me. I knew nothing about love. We were not shown love or taught to love. We were told to be tough and to fight. I think it was just my parents' way of protecting us. My childhood experiences led me right inside the prison walls of anger.

Being a fighter became my state of mind. Every time I tell my testimony, most of the people listening seem to wear the same facial expression, with eyes of disbelief. I was enraged. I was such a fool. I could never control my anger, neither as a kid nor as a grown man. I was the toughest, yet the shortest, of all my friends.

From Iraq to America

In America, I loved to fight, especially with the bullies on the block. I was so proud to know that no one dared to challenge my friends or me. I have so many memories of beating up kids that they all kind of blend together now.

I came to the United States at 11 years of age, speaking Aramaic and Arabic. Aramaic, or what we call Sourath, is the language Jesus Christ spoke—but for years, there was nothing truly Christlike about me.

In the '60s, the government of Iraq was being overthrown. My brother Salah got involved in politics, and one night the army picked up four of my brothers. My dad got scared, so we fled. We actually had our legal papers to move to the United States in the 1940s, but my father loved Iraq and never really wanted to leave.

In the 1960s, Chaldeans were buying businesses from earlier immigrants, such as the Jewish and Italian communities. Once my brother got involved in the government, my dad knew it was time to go.

LOCKED IN ANGER

The pre-Saddam Hussein regime even tried to entice us to come back by offering my brother a high position, but my father refused. We were living in peace in America for the most part; he said we were done with Iraq, so we stayed. It was in the late '60s, and Iraq's Ba'ath party came into power just as we were starting a new life in a new home.

We followed Chaldeans who immigrated to the United States in the early 1900s for jobs at Ford Motor Company, paying $5 a day. When we relocated to the United States, we lived on the west side of Detroit on San Juan Street. It was ethnically diverse, but we felt like aliens. We didn't speak English. We looked like total foreigners. People used to throw bricks and garbage pails at our windows, often breaking the glass. I worried about my family all the time—my little brothers and, of course, my mom.

We lived on that street for less than a year, but during that time, I became resentful. I don't think those people really hated us; they were simply ignorant. They looked at us as if we were some sort of weird creatures and just wanted to attack us. Those were difficult months and such a bad first impression of America for my family.

Recounting those early years has become a staple in my testimony. The years that I struggled fueled my anger. I looked for the jerks. I really did. I was waiting just to pound on someone. Bullies were an easy target. They gave me an excuse to intimidate and attack. It wasn't like I accidentally walked into madness and chaos; I attracted it. I sought it, and I wanted to be a part of it because the rage inside of me needed an outlet.

My family eventually moved to another part of Detroit, where a small population of Christian Iraqis known as Chaldeans lived. At one time, we lived about a block away from where the Michigan State Fair used to be held, just off of Woodward and 7 Mile. This was just one mile

FREEDOM BEHIND BARS

south of the suburbs of Oakland County. Back then, the 8 Mile divide was a major political issue. There was a lot of racial tension, and that was shortly before the Detroit riots. This area near 7 Mile, just across from the affluent neighborhood of Palmer Woods and Palmer Park, grew into a substantial Chaldean population that eventually sustained its own church for several years.

We arrived in the U.S. about a year prior to the Detroit riots and before protesters gathered in the streets to show their opposition to the Vietnam War. This was around the time Motown Music was climbing the charts, and the Beatles were touring the country, making stops in Detroit.

I wasn't paying attention to any of it. I walked around with broken English and a bad attitude. My dad got a job working at Carl's Chop House in Detroit. He recruited other Chaldeans to work at the restaurant. The managers and owners loved them there. Chaldeans are and have always been hard workers.

Trying to assimilate into American life wasn't easy for me. Looking back, it seems so strange to me. I actually did really well in school. I got good grades. I used to get so excited about report cards. However, no one ever looked at them or attended a conference with my teachers. No one helped me with homework. I was a good student who got into a lot of trouble because no one was paying attention.

The Lion and the Lamb

I know some of that anger stemmed from feeling ignored. I got lost in the herd, being the 7th child of 11 kids. We had family gatherings, dinners, and holidays, but no one was ever treated as an individual. I am not blaming my parents, but it is a reality. They did what they knew best. The reality was, no one took the time to know me or guide me.

LOCKED IN ANGER

I realized at an early age that my life was different from the neighborhood kids in Detroit. We grew up in this foreign land on our own. We never went to baseball games with our dad. My dad never played catch with us outside. We were living in America but weren't really living the American life.

While other kids were playing basketball, I went to work. I was just 12 years old, stocking shelves at a party store in Detroit not far from where the police headquarters are today. I took a bus near my home, got off a mile away from the store, and walked the rest of the way. My feet often hurt, but there was no reason to cry about it—no one was listening. I walked in the snow or puddles of rain, and my feet swelled.

We celebrated a lot of family events, but never a birthday. I don't think anyone ever remembered my birthday. We didn't get birthday presents. I remember hugging my dad on my wedding day, and he turned red. I thought he was going to have a heart attack. It was so foreign to him.

Although much was missing, I cared for my family. Even though it was never taught or expressed growing up, nestled inside the anger was love for my parents and siblings. I knew my brothers and sisters would always have my back; we worked together. The joy I felt being around my family that was buried down deep was the virtue that would eventually release me from the prison of anger. I had to learn prudence first and then came joy. That would be years later.

On top of never feeling loved as a child, we were punished often. We were yelled at if we ever got out of line, but we were never acknowledged for doing anything right. No one ever had a problem telling you when they were disappointed in you, but never when they were proud of you.

Unknowingly then, but without harboring resentment today, that lack of nurturing probably ignited some of the anger that lived inside me. My parents did what they believed was best, especially as immigrants to America. My mom worked so hard. She cooked, cleaned, and did everything around the house. I don't think she even had a good night's sleep or even enough sleep. She did what was expected of moms in the villages of Iraq, and she was just doing that in America too. She didn't realize different things were expected of moms here.

Without even realizing it, a crazed and angry lion was growing inside the lamb. I would later learn through Scripture that the things that proceed out of the mouth come from the heart. Why would anything but hate come from my mouth? It was hatred that filled my heart.

While my dad and older brothers worked, I was hunting down a bully; his name was Billy. He stood more than 6 feet tall and had bright red hair. He used to torment every weak kid around. I loved looking for him just to fight him.

It was the early 1970s now; one night, I was driving my '68 Plymouth Road Runner. I was 16 years old now. I had it all rigged up as much I could without my older brother taking notice. He would have been angry if he found out I rigged my car for speed.

I pulled up at John R Street near 8 Mile Road in Detroit. My friend Ray was with me, drinking Pepsi out of an 8-ounce glass bottle. Stopped at the light next to us was none other than Billy. His car windows were rolled down, and, without hesitation, I grabbed the bottle and threw it right at his face, and POW! Man, it just smacked him in the face, soda pop spraying out everywhere. He tried to chase us down, but my rig was too fast.

LOCKED IN ANGER

This was the kind of stuff that excited me because I could do something about my rage. I grew up in a Catholic home and even went to Catholic school for part of my life. I didn't understand that God was calling us to be joyful because I was too busy being angry.

I am just 5"6" tall, but my anger pushed my shoulders back and created a tense and stern face. Happiness was not on my mind or in my heart. My face was an expression of my thoughts, and they were of being irritated most of the time.

In my early 20s, I went into the grocery business because it was a natural fit for immigrants. I followed in the footsteps of my older brothers, who followed in the footsteps of Chaldean immigrants before them.

The first store we worked at as brothers was in the early 1970s in Detroit on Schoolcraft and Wyoming; it was an old A&P Supermarket. That store eventually sold, and we bought others in Detroit. All the stores we owned were in the city.

The fighting kid inside me simply grew up into a man even more enraged. In fact, customer service for me included all-out brawls with many Detroiters who frequented my store. I would lose sleep as I planned revenge for anyone who had insulted me that day. I didn't know the truth. If you know the truth, you will know that a wise person does not have to prove anything to anyone because he is confident in himself as a child of Christ.

I didn't know then that we need to look at our anger directly in the mirror and assess the damage it is causing. I used to fight customers at the store to the point I would lose all control. I would reach such a high state of rage that I would eventually snap and find myself on top of a customer, beating him down to the ground. Some fights started in

FREEDOM BEHIND BARS

one area of the store, and I would later realize I was in a totally different aisle, pummeling someone.

I lost focus on what was going on during a fight. I had customers in chokeholds—guys with arms as big as bowling balls and my anger pumped the adrenaline through my body. I have thrown cans of food and wedged my knees into people. So many times, I would snap out of the rage by hearing my brother Hani screaming, "Have you lost your mind?"

My brothers knew all too well my rage. They witnessed so many of my fights. When I heard my brother Hani come near me, I would look at him and say, "Akhoni, (brother) step aside," because I didn't want him to get hurt.

I remember one time when a customer—I loved her; she was a good woman—begged me to stop beating up this one man in the parking lot. I can still see her face today. "Please, Tom, stop!" she cried. "Please, stop!"

Aging out of my teenage years into adulthood, I eventually got married and had four kids. I had an arranged marriage. My father picked her for me. It was odd because, at that point, I considered myself an American, yet I allowed my parents to arrange my marriage. It was common practice for Chaldean parents to find spouses for their children. It wasn't a foreign concept to me but still odd now that I was in America.

To the world, I was living the American Dream. I had a business, a nice home, a family; in short, everything every immigrant comes to America to achieve. In reality, my life was hell. I didn't know it then. It was all normal to me.

LOCKED IN ANGER

That was the lion inside me. My wife and kids knew the lamb. When I was around family, I could silence the roar. If it was possible for an angry man to find joy, I found it at home. It was now the early '80s. The kids, four of them, were young, ages 1 to 8.

Turns out my parents picked a good wife. Sue and I had a fantastic marriage. We often took trips, including a trip to a favorite northern Michigan hotel with a swimming pool. Every Wednesday night, we had a date night. I loved buying her flowers. I bought them about twice a week. I would pick her up and carry her to bed. The kids climbed all over me and would cheer and laugh when I did pushups while they sat on my back. My cousins used to make fun of me, but I loved being married, and I adored my kids. I wanted to give Sue and my children the best life possible.

When people would ask me how life was going, I would joke and say, "Life is very tough. I go home every day. I beat the wife. I bite the dog." My wife used to say, "Don't kid around with people like that. They really believe you. They don't really know you."

The reality is that no one really knew me. I didn't really know myself because I didn't know God. I was the lost sheep whom the Shepherd went looking for, and, thank God, He found him.

A Reflection on the Prison Cell of Anger

Today, when I give my testimony, I am often asked about righteous anger. There are situations when being angry is appropriate.

There is just anger and unjust anger. Things in life will upset us. Turn on the news on any given night, and a calm, gentle person will become upset. Maybe that's you—someone locked in anger because of things that happened a long time ago.

Scripture led me out of the prison cell of anger. "Be angry but do not sin; don't let the sunset on your anger" (Eph. 4:26). I let the sunset on my anger every day. That is a big difference. The anger fueled my rage, and I was on a path of ruin.

If we stay angry, we become prisoners of it. If we let anger consume us, it will make us sick; we will not be able to sleep, and sometimes we will make bad decisions because we can't discern what is just and unjust anger. I made the decision to blow up my competitor's business, and I ended up in prison.

There are examples of just anger in Scripture. When Jesus was angry in the temple, He made a three-ply whip out of rope. The Gospel of John tells us:

*"He found in the temple area those who sold oxen, sheep and doves, as well as the moneychangers seated there. He made a whip out of cords and drove them all out of the temple area, with the sheep and oxen, and spilled the coins of the moneychangers and overturned their tables, and to those who sold doves He said, **take** these out of here, and stop making my Father's house a marketplace" (John 2:13-17).*

His love for holiness is what led Jesus to just anger.

I think about all the things that have angered me over the years, and they pale in comparison to the offenses others have faced. For example, I think back to January 2018, when Rachael Denhollander was the last of 156 victims to make a statement against sentenced sex abuser and former USA Gymnastics doctor Larry Nassar. She didn't seek revenge. She didn't even display anger in her testimony. She stood up with courage and forgave the monster. Nassar was sentenced to 175 years for sexually abusing girls and young women for years. In this highly publicized case about a former Michigan State University sports physician, Rachael Denhollander

LOCKED IN ANGER

showed grace she credits God for giving her. She points to the bible and to God in her testimony.

Reading what she said in court reminded me that having that kind of grace is what knowing Christ enables you to do. I did not know Him, so not only was I unable to forgive those who hurt me, but I also set out to destroy them and almost destroyed myself in the process.

We must first know God and know the truth if we want to be released; I found my way out through reading the Word of God. I encourage you to do the same. Psychologists and researchers have studied the emotion of anger for decades. Psychology has explained anger as the natural emotion created in a fight-or-flight situation by the physiology of your mind and body. When you sense a threat, your mind generates fear and anger. The fear you generate is part of a flight response from your physiology. Anger is the emotional energy you generate for the fight against that perceived threat. What can be confusing is that your mind creates fear and anger even when the threat is imagined.

So, you could say that my mind was confused. My anger gave a short-statured guy the guts to take on the meanest kids on the block. Perhaps fear generated the flight response or a response to fight. I was locked in the prison walls of fear, too, but I will get into that later.

Scripture teaches us that "A fool vents off his anger quickly, but a wise man holds it back" (Prov. 29:11). I was a fool. In Proverbs 12:16, we learn that the fool immediately shows his anger, but the shrewd man passes over an insult. Here is a person who can't control his or her anger, and it leads to irrational decisions and all kinds of trouble; my irrational thinking led me to blow up my competition. I literally ignited bombs.

FREEDOM BEHIND BARS

Prisons are filled with angry people. I know. I lived with these people for nearly two decades. Like a lot of people, I needed a course in anger management, but, most importantly, I needed to find my faith and justice in God. I needed to find Jesus to be released from my anger.

When we read from scripture in the book of Ephesians, we learn that we are called to be Christlike; we must put on love and compassion because our God is love. Our anger should only be used to do righteous things and not be used in a violent way.

Did I have the right to be upset because a customer stole something? Sure. Did I have the right to beat him unconscious? No. It was only after reading Scripture that the anger began to dissipate. I read the Bible, and truth began to set in. When I started to read the Bible, I really didn't know-how. Like any book, I started in the beginning. The Old Testament is where I found a way to release my anger.

Scripture shows us when anger is appropriate. In the Book of Psalms, we learn about righteous anger: "God is a righteous judge, yes, a God that hath indignation every day" (Psalms 7:11). But that did not apply to me. My anger was not righteous or justified. Ask yourself if your anger is justified.

You must first be honest about the anger you hold inside. In Ephesians, the question is asked: Is your anger leading you to sin? For me, the answer was yes. I was out for blood.

If you are truly locked in anger, the only way you will get out is first recognizing that you are living inside of it. Out-of-control anger can be irreparable without God's help. Anger also becomes a sin when the angry one refuses to be pacified, holds a grudge, or keeps it all inside. I was certainly harboring it.

Scripture shows us how to handle our anger. While in prison, I learned to use Scripture to heal and unlock the doors. "If we

LOCKED IN ANGER

confess our sins, He is faithful and just to forgive us our sins and to cleanse us from all unrighteousness" (1 John 1:9).

Confession is a tough one for many people, including Catholics. Rachael Denhollander encouraged her abuser to repent. As a Christian, she knows how powerful and freeing this can be, even if she doesn't practice the Catholic Sacrament.

Perhaps it's tough because it's misunderstood. The Sacrament of Reconciliation is an important aspect of Catholicism. Jesus Christ, in His abundant love and mercy, established the Sacrament of Confession so that we, as sinners, can obtain forgiveness for our sins and reconcile with God and the Church. The Sacrament washes us clean and renews us in Christ.

You acknowledge and confess it to yourself, to God, and to those who were victims of your wrath. I justified my anger by believing people offended me, but I later learned that we could free ourselves of the anger by seeing God in our trials. In the Book of James, it reads, "Consider it pure joy, my brothers and sisters, whenever you face trials of many kinds because you know that the testing of your faith produces perseverance. Let perseverance finish its work so that you may be mature and complete, not lacking anything" (James. 1: 2-4).

I faced trials. I struggled to adjust to this country. I never felt important or loved growing up. I started working as a young kid. I never got to truly enjoy a childhood. So yeah, I was angry. I was able to take my sinful life and turn it into something for the greater good—for God.

When Scripture tells us to "Be angry and do not sin; do not let the sun go down on your anger," it points to the fact that God is sovereign over every circumstance and person that crosses our path. Nothing happens to us that He does not allow.

FREEDOM BEHIND BARS

Though God does allow bad things to happen, He is always faithful to redeem them for the good of His people. Reflecting on this truth until it moves from our heads to our hearts will alter how we react to those who hurt us. It took me nearly a decade in prison before the truth transcended from my mind to my soul. I lived inside the prison walls, not only physically but also spiritually within myself.

Anger can also prompt people to seek revenge, which it did for me throughout my life. But we are not to ever be playing God. Also, in the Book of Genesis, we read that "God is righteous and just, and we can trust Him who knows all and sees all to act justly" (Gen. 18:25).

Anger is one of the Seven Deadly Sins. In the Sermon on the Mount, Jesus identified anger as a violation of the 5th Commandment and as endangering one's eternal soul: "You have heard that it was said to the men of old, 'You shall not kill; and whoever kills shall be liable to judgment.' But I say to you that everyone who is angry with his brother shall be liable to judgment" (Matthew 5:21-22).

The virtue that will release us from anger is prudence. With cautiousness, we make better decisions. When anger is released, we can find joy. Are you joyful missionary disciples of the Lord? That is what we are called to be—joyful. I had no discipline or control over my anger.

Immaturity and our fallen nature often create impulsive behavior, which can be sinful. We are told in Ephesians to act and not to react. I had a reactive nature. When you are prudent, you are not reactive. You stop thinking about what you are doing. I never used the principle of counting to 10 to calm my nerves before handling the situation. Today, I have learned to pray silently to myself when I feel anger coming on.

LOCKED IN ANGER

Today, I discern all important matters. I find joy in Jesus. I focus on the virtue of prudence when I have to make a decision, and I know that a certain situation is making me angry. I use much better judgment because I ask for the Holy Spirit to guide me. I learned to rejoice in the Lord. He triumphed. He is our Savior, and that exhilarates us and brings jubilation.

The years leading to prison and during the first 10 years there, I was impulsive, and my anger took over. Thus, I created bigger problems. I neither established boundaries nor did I practice discernment, as we are taught in Scripture. I was not cautious in my decision-making.

Part of being released is evaluating friendships and the people you surround yourself with on a regular basis. Who are you attracting in your life? Sometimes, our desire to release ourselves from anger leads us to recognize that certain people are unsafe for us. It did that for me. We can still forgive them, but we may choose not to re-enter the relationship. We cannot control how others act or respond, but we can make the changes in our hearts to act with love.

The key to releasing ourselves out of the prison of anger is to convert the feeling to joy. We must look for what brings us joy, example God, our family, and all of our blessings. I had to learn to love my enemies. I had to learn to find joy in everyday life. That is the ultimate virtue we need to discover in the midst of our anger. We do that by focusing on using reason.

I had to be prudent. I had to see the right thing to do and choose the right means for achieving it. Prudence means applying good moral principles to particular situations, assisting us to know what to seek and what to avoid. Prudence is necessary to seek the Common Good for all.

FREEDOM BEHIND BARS

Overcoming anger and a temper is not accomplished overnight. But through prayer, scripture, and confidence of the Trinity, ungodly anger can be defused. I may have allowed anger to become entrenched in my life by habit, but I later realized that by practicing the faith, I was released from the prison of anger. With each day, I was getting closer to glorifying God in all that I did.

Do you find yourself in these scenarios that could cause anger?

- The injustices of the world
- Being wrongly accused of something you did not do
- Someone hurting your business or career
- Losing your job or losing out on a job promotion
- Losing money
- Being jealous of someone
- Having relationship problems

Reflective Questions:

These are questions we could ask ourselves if we are locked in the prison of anger.

- Are you locked inside anger? If so, how?
- Are you acting like a fool? If so, how?
- Do you vent your anger quickly?
- Where has being angry gotten you?
- How can you bring the virtue of prudence into your life?

If you are locked in anger, here are more Scripture verses to meditate on:

LOCKED IN ANGER

Get Rid of all bitterness, rage, and anger, brawling and slander, along with every form of malice (Ephesians 4:31).

But now you must put them all away: anger, fury, malice, slander, and obscene language out of your mouths (Colossians 3:8).

"The man of violent temper pays the penalty; even if you rescue him, you will have it to do again" (Proverbs 19:19).

"Refrain from anger and forsake wrath! Do not fret; it tends only to evil" (Psalms 37:8).

Chapter 2

LOCKED IN HATE

Finding Freedom in the Virtue of Love

Confess your faults one to another, and pray one for another, that you may be healed. The effectual fervent prayer of a righteous man avails much" -James 5:16.

±

I remember telling a part of my story to Teresa Tomeo, the host of Catholic Connection on Ave Maria Radio and EWTN, Global Catholic Network; it was the part that ultimately led me to prison.

It was one of the station's on-air drives, and I was invited to share my testimony. I started to tell my story, and, like everyone else, she looked at me in amazement; she had this expression on her face that said, "There is no way this guy is for real."

I told her, "You need to understand my state of mind to fully grasp how I landed behind bars." When I hear myself tell this story today, I am perplexed at the complete absurdity of it all. What the heck was I thinking? The fact is, I wasn't.

There was really nothing righteous about me as a young man. I was locked in anger and eventually hate and consumed by revenge. In my mind, the competition was going to pay. I was not going to let them ruin my business.

I continued without acknowledging Teresa's look of surprise. I tried burning down my competitor's store four times. Yup—*four times*.

Teresa's eyes bulged out a bit, and she looked to others in the room, seeking affirmation that I was telling the truth. The truth was that I was locked in the prison of hate and didn't know it. This hate is what landed me in prison for nearly 16 years. I am not the person I used to be, and sometimes, when I tell this part of my testimony, I am unrecognizable to myself.

Like I did so many times while telling my story, I took Teresa and her listeners back to the late '80s. On a typical Tuesday night, I went to the club I often frequented in Southfield to hang out with the guys, have dinner, and play cards. Southfield is a suburb about 20 miles north of downtown Detroit.

I hung out at the club so much because I needed to establish an alibi. I orchestrated it in such a way that many witnesses would attest to seeing me at the club. Every time, I managed to sneak out without anyone paying attention. I always called a friend to help bomb my competitor; these were often Johnny and Ray, and I had my car packed with explosives. Each time I attempted to burn down my competitor's business, I started out the night at the club to so people could see me.

For the sake of protecting their identity, my competitors in this book are the Mansour family. It's not their real last name. On the date of the crime, my friends and I got to the store in the evening, after hours, and broke the doors. We burned the store from the inside after everybody went home. Then I called one of my friends from the club. I wanted to brag about my escapade of the night. It was quite sick to think about it, but I was proud of what I did and wanted to share the news with friends.

I picked up a friend that night, and we drove to the crime scene—to the store I had just set on fire. We sat watching the police and the fire department try to put out the flames. I was hoping, actually praying, it would burn to the ground, but it didn't. My friend looked at me and asked, "Well, who did this?" I looked at him and answered sarcastically, "Hello! Who do you think?"

My friend was ecstatic. What I remember is that everybody wanted me to burn that store down. As a matter of fact, the night before, I had one of the guys from the neighborhood approach me. He was like, "Tom, these guys are such jerks; we got a party store, and we sell cigarettes, and they're even putting the cigarettes on sale. I wish somebody would burn them down. I'll donate the first thousand."

Nobody liked them in the area, as I often explained in my testimony, or at least that is what I wanted to believe. All I saw were store owners competing with everyone around them. The next day the fire was all the talk. The other store owner I had talked to the night before asked, "Who did you give the first thousand to?'" He didn't know that I set the store on fire.

However, many people suspected me. Our two families had already been feuding. I was the only one from the Naemi family who would engage in the fighting. My brothers, who were my business partners, stayed out of the feud and never knew what I was planning.

I got questioned by the police, but I had so many witnesses tell them that I was at the club in Southfield. No one realized I had left.

The two stores were only a quarter of a mile apart. Since we competed for the same dollar, we fought all the time. Several incidences of fighting happened in the months prior to me firebombing the store.

FREEDOM BEHIND BARS

I was told that my competitor's butcher referred a meat wrapper clerk to me; apparently, she was there to sabotage our business. We hired her not knowing that they suggested she apply for the job. One day, she got a phone call, and my brother Hani accidentally answered her line. We had a four-line telephone system. He was trying to dial out from another line when he answered a call she was on. He supposedly heard her say, "I'm going to mess these people up, and I'm going to send all the customers to your store."

They allegedly put the meat wrapper to work in the seafood department as a plant to hurt our business. Even I had a hard time believing it at first. Nobody is going to be that low to do something like that, I thought. Who knows, really? Look what I did.

Our store was called Seamaan's. We bought it from another family with that last name and never changed it. It was profitable despite the competition, and I had vengeance inside. I wanted to investigate for myself if the new meat wrapper was a spy. I decided to go to my competitor's store one day with my manager, Hoss. We went there to see what was going on, and that's when the big brother got nervous. I walked in and said, "You guys want to do business in a nice way, or you guys want to play dirty?"

The oldest brother of the family looked at me and said, "Well, why don't you come on in the back?"

Already filled with anger, it didn't take much to move me toward complete hatred for this family. He snatched my wrist, and I pulled it from him. "Listen, take your hands off of me!" I shouted, repeating: "Do you guys want to do business in a nice way, or do you guys want to play games? Because we can play. Oh yeah, brother, we can play."

He grabbed my wrist again, insisting we take the talk into the back room of the store.

I hit him with such force that he flew across the room. From the corner of my eye, I saw another person running toward me. I quickly turned around and punched him. I just kept throwing punches at anyone who came my way and eventually jumped over the meat counter. The hate I had inside was in full force.

I felt a hand on my back and, without even looking to see who it was, I flung around and kicked the guy on his forehead. I was hitting and kicking everyone around me. I was in a place of complete rage. As I explained earlier, when my hate turned into a state of rage, it was as if something else took hold of my body. I was no longer in control. I had absolutely no fear, and I never stopped to think. I just reacted. I really was like the Hulk; I just never turned green or grew taller and bigger.

Before I realized it, I saw a group of guys rushing toward me. While in this anger, I never stopped to think of the consequences or even about getting hurt. Despite the fact that they outnumbered me, I continued to throw products and punches. One of them picked up a case of corn to throw at me. Every time he would come near me, I'd hit him one time, he'd back away, and he'd come again. "Move, move, let me hit him!" he would say, and I hit him about four times. Then I heard the voice of a third Mansour brother yelling, "STOP!"

My cousin Nick ran in to help. Another guy grabbed me from the back, but I once again managed to turn around and punch him. I ducked, and the punch caught Nick in the face. Nick started bleeding. I dropkicked the guy a second time. Boom! I said, "Here, that's for you," I said, I kicked him again. "Here," the second I dropkicked him another time. I was worried. Man, we fought from the back in the store, but for one second, I actually got worried."

My thought was always that these people didn't know who they were messing with, and I warned them I would be back. "You guys don't know who I am. You'll find out; I'll be your worst nightmare," I told the brothers.

The Mansour brothers ended up in the hospital after that fight.

Firebombed

Weeks had passed since that store fight. It was the summer of 1986. The Mansours built their store back up after I set it on fire, but the hate and competition between us never stopped.

I was ready to make good on my promise. I was once again ready for payback. The busiest times of the year in the store business were always the 4th of July and Thanksgiving. The day before Thanksgiving and the 3rd of July were the busiest days in the supermarket business and probably still are.

I got three of my "boys from the hood" to bring me about 26 more boys; they were all football players. I offered them $200 each and set out a plan for them to go to the Mansour store. The orders were that no one walked out. I wanted everyone sent to the hospital. I instructed each to walk in with two or three customers, so it didn't appear suspicious. I wanted them to pretend to be shoppers.

I directed them to separate aisles around the store and start fighting in the glass aisle, where pickles and ketchup were shelved; the football players did as I instructed.

Later that day, I was back at the store, and my brother Hani started telling me about a fight he heard broke out at the Mansour's. I

LOCKED IN HATE

acted shocked. "Customers are coming in and saying there's like 50 police cars, and they dumped displays and damaged the store," said Hani.

"Well, you know those people; they're always messing with people," I replied. "They're known for stealing from people, and they probably did something crappy to someone, and something went wrong." Hani looked at me while cutting the meat with an expression of suspicion.

"You didn't have nothing to do with it, did you?"

"Come on, Hani, we got work to do," I said. "We don't have time for this BS."

Hani left. I never told my brothers what I did or any of the things I used to do. My wife never had a clue, either, and of course, my kids were just babies. I heard recounts of that day from others later. People started running into the bathroom to hide. I figured at the time that the score was even. In my head, it was all justified. My competitors were messing with me for months, sending me messages through other people, like, "We're going to cut off your water," and this and that. So, I had to send them a message back—much stronger than theirs.

Although I claimed my competitors copied my store ads, it didn't bother me as much as when all of them wanted to fight me. My ego was on the line. A few more days passed, and I received a call from some guy in the community. We will call him Al.

"You could have had these guys killed," Al said to me. "My cousin probably lost his hearing on his left side. What'd you do?"

"I didn't do anything," I replied. "I just gave them a piece of me; I taught them some manners; you know. They can't all jump on one guy who comes in the store. Now, they're going to know."

A few more days passed when one of the brothers called me to say they wanted peace, and I figured peace was good. They would leave me alone, and I would leave them alone. Well, that lasted about three weeks until the Mansours recovered from the fight and got out of the hospital. One night, they called me right before the store closed for the night.

I used to close the store between 9 and 9:15 p.m. after I finished checking out all the cashiers, their units, and the deposits. As I was finalizing the night's deposits, I saw cars pull up in the parking lot—a white Buick, a yellow Camaro, and a red car. I didn't recall the exact make of it. They called me on the phone.

"Come on outside, man. We got something for you," they said.

"Oh boy! You guys, you got brave again, huh? You didn't have enough last time? You want more?" I asked.

"Oh, you know, we're going to kill you," they replied. "We're going to even the score."

"All right. I'll be right out," I said.

I opened the safe inside the store office and pulled out an Uzi. I planned to spray them in the parking lot. I walked out with my gun. As soon as they saw me unlocking the door with an Uzi in my hand, they took off.

I was thinking, "Okay, these people are really stupid. They just don't know when to quit." I figured, let's escalate it a little bit. Let me give them Plan B. Now, we have to really burn this store down.

It took about five months for them to rebuild after I torched it; they remodeled the store. The insurance company paid. Police came to my store to question me, but nothing ever came of it.

LOCKED IN HATE

Even while being questioned by the cops, I was thinking, "I need to do this again."

I looked at the cops and treated them as if they were being stupid, even questioning me. "Come on, man, I was at the club in Southfield. A thousand people saw me," I said.

They asked a lot of people, and they all told them that I was at the club until 4 that morning. I used to change my clothes and get in the van and go. As I said, no one ever realized I left for a while. A few more weeks had passed, and I heard through the community that the Mansours were bad-mouthing me, so I planned another fire attack. I figured they would never expect it.

The second time I set the store on fire was around 4 o'clock in the afternoon. I hired a guy from a fake roofing company with a fake name on his pickup truck. The guy placed a ladder on the side of the building and climbed up. He sprayed the whole roof with gasoline and threw a flare on it.

There were 25 gallons of gasoline on the roof, and it burned. Police and firefighters arrived. Although panicked, everyone was able to run out. This time only the roof burned, and they fixed it. After that incident, they gated the entire store. They closed it off and fenced the roof. I couldn't find a way to get back in. However, even though they had barbed wire around the store, I knew I was going to find a way to get them again.

My competitors repeatedly called to threaten me. I was becoming furious, and the rage was brewing because they were really messing with my ego. I tried for a third time to blow up the store. I got this 16-and-a-half-pound bomb with a timer; I hired this lady and showed her how to connect and disconnect the bomb.

FREEDOM BEHIND BARS

I instructed her to go in the store and shop and then to put the bomb behind toilet paper or Pampers because they're big boxes and it wouldn't be spotted. I explained to her that once she set the bomb there and pulled the pin out very gently, the timer would start and go around for one hour. By then, they'd have plenty of time to close the store. It would be after 10 when the timer ran out. I planned to have somebody call them, tell them to leave the store because there was a bomb inside, and if they didn't believe it, they could find it in the tissue aisle behind a Pampers box.

The woman went into the store and did everything I told her to do. The timer ticked so loudly that an employee found it and started screaming, "There's a bomb! There's a bomb!"

Everyone panicked. They started cutting off the lights, and customers ran out. The police were called, and they took the bomb to Belle Isle on the Detroit River and detonated it.

That was nearly $11,000 down the river. It was $5,600 for the bomb and $5,000 for the lady. Yeah, that stuff cost money. I figured the scare was worth the money, but it wasn't good enough. I went to the club, where people were talking about the bomb at the Mansours store.

"You know, the bomb squad, they put the bomb on Belle Isle, and it blew up, and a bunch of fish came out of the water," one guy at the club told me.

"What are you doing to do?" I replied. "Things happen. Good things happen to bad people, and bad things happen to good people."

Following this incident, I started to get calls that there were plans to kill me. I was told a sum of $25,000 was offered to someone

LOCKED IN HATE

to take me out. My cousins and friends kept telling me that the Mansours planned to have me killed. I later heard they hired a couple of kids from the neighborhood. Now, do I know that any of this was really true? I don't know. All I know is what people told me.

The rivalry between us was well known in the community, but were they really trying to kill me? At that time, I was a ferocious animal looking for prey. I was waiting for a reason to kill. Whether it was true or not didn't matter. I hated these guys.

The Guns Ablaze

It was 1987. I used to go to work at 6 in the morning. On this particular day, it was after the 15th when business slowed down a little bit, so I decided to sleep for a few hours. The first two weeks of the month in Detroit were always very busy for any business because that is when customers were issued food stamps for the month. I asked Hani to open the store that morning.

I used to park my car in the same spot every day. The door was in the center of the building, and I would park my car right in the northwest corner of the store. I drove a Cadillac sedan back then. That day, there were a bunch of cars parked there, so I parked in the middle of the parking lot on the end.

I walked from the car to the middle of the building, and these two guys came up to me. I looked at them and saw guns in their hands. I threw myself down, and they started shooting. I always carried a gun, so I started shooting back. Those inside, including my brother and cousin, heard the shooting. They all came out with guns, and we started chasing them. We lost them somewhere by the cemetery about a quarter mile down from the store.

FREEDOM BEHIND BARS

At this point, I was crazed. I just kept telling myself, "Somebody was going to die, and it wasn't going to be me."

A Fight Brewing

During the next few days, owners of the businesses in the neighborhood were telling me how the Mansours were cursing and cussing me out. Rocky, another store owner, specifically came to tell me how they wanted to kill me. They hated Rocky, too, and used to mess with him.

It was my understanding that all the stores in this particular area of the east side of Detroit were affected by this competitor. The competitor sat in the middle of three other stores, but I was the only one who fought back.

I drafted another plan. It was Memorial Day weekend in 1987. I closed the store early, and instead of going home, I went to the local coffee shop on Woodward near 7 Mile, where I knew the Mansours often hung out. As soon as I walked in, everyone stopped talking and stared. They knew I never frequented that coffee shop, and they also knew about my ongoing feud with the Mansours.

I sat down and ordered the kabob. My cousin George was with me, but he had no idea what I was about to do. He didn't even know why he was there. I said nothing to him about it. While we were eating, two guys came up to me and started saying that the Mansours were cursing me out and talking about my family.

A fight inside my mind began to brew, and I was determined to do them in. I could feel my body turning monster green, and my face was burning the angrier I became. I sat there for two hours, waiting for the Mansours to show up. As I was paying the bill, they walked in. They had about six people with them. I thought, "Thank you, Lord."

LOCKED IN HATE

I know. Can you believe I was thanking God for these guys walking in so I could kill them? I was so sick in the head. I could tell that they saw me. As soon as they walked in, I turned around. I was now completely engulfed in rage. Never afraid of anybody, I was ready to attack. They walked about 20 feet and got extremely nervous and turned pale.

I was watching them like an animal preying on its dinner. They got ready to leave, and I walked up to the door and locked it. I then walked over to them, and they started to scram. They were looking to run for cover and began to panic. The two brothers who talked to me earlier tried to stop me. They all knew I was about to lose it. "Tom, it's not worth it," one of them shouted.

A couple of people tried to stop the fight, but they knew I wanted this fight to happen. In my mind, it had to happen. I heard the other of the two brothers yell, "Tom, please don't do anything. Nothing is worth it!"

"Get out!" I yelled. "Move aside, man. I don't need no backup."

I stood there, and they all stopped.

"Where are you going?" I asked.

"What?" one of them asked.

"Where are you going?" I repeated. "Aren't you guys going to come here and make threats? Tell people how you're going to kill somebody? Aren't you guys going to get brave here today?"

"Look, man, we have no beef with you," one of the Mansour brothers said.

"Oh, you don't?" I shot back. "Didn't you guys come here

FREEDOM BEHIND BARS

swearing at people and claiming somebody burned your store down?" I shouted louder. "Lord, who burned your store down, you piece of crap? Who burned it? Didn't you guys do an insurance job so you could remodel that store?"

I could see the older brother starting to panic. I didn't know if he was trying to pull his gun or not, so I pulled out both guns I had with me, and everyone hit the floor. I walked up to the Mansours and cocked the gun. I had a .380 pistol. "Didn't I tell you I would be your worst nightmare?" I asked.

Adam, the owner of the restaurant, came running to block my bullet. He jumped right in front of my gun. "Don't shoot! Don't shoot!" he yelled. "Please, Tom, don't shoot in my place!"

"Adam, man, get out of the way!" I shouted.

During these years, I allowed every expletive to come tumbling out of my mouth. I knew every swear word in the English, Arabic, and Aramaic languages, and I used them all—all the time. As I was hovering over the Mansours with a cocked gun, I freely used those words.

As I stood with the gun in my hand, I was thinking I would kill them and then get in my car and take the tunnel over to Windsor, Canada. From there, I would get on a plane and fly to Iraq. These were the crazy thoughts going on in my head. My thought was interrupted by Adam.

"Tom, don't, don't! Please, calm down!" he begged.

"Okay, man, you calm down."

"Take it outside, Tom, please."

"We got to finish this once and for all. Somebody has got to die today, and it isn't going to be me."

"Tom, I promise, I'll bring them outside. I give you, my word."

"Okay, let's do it outside. They're going to die today."

I followed Adam outside. As soon as I stepped out the door, I heard the door slam shut, and someone on the other side locked it. They locked themselves in.

I heard Adam talking from the other side of the door. "What's wrong with you?" he asked. "I've never seen you act stupid before. I've known you for a long time. What's gotten into you?"

"Nothing, Adam," I said. "This is none of your business. We need to solve this, me and them, today."

"Calm down, Tom."

"I am calm. I've got to do this today. We got to finish this."

Someone opened the door. Nobody came out. I walked in, and I realized the only reason they opened the door was that they let the Mansours go out the back door. They were gone. "Where are those jerks? Where are they?"

"They ran out the back door," someone shouted.

"Adam, you shouldn't have done that," I said, looking his way.

I looked outside, and one of the Mansours' cousins tried to hit me with a case of corn. His hands were shaking. He was trying to put the key in the door of his white Buick Park Avenue, but he was so nervous, that he couldn't open it. "I'm going to kill you guys!" I screamed.

I ran after one of the brothers, and he took off, so the only one left was the guy with the key in his hand. I began chasing the oldest brother, running back into the other coffee shop. I don't know what he said, but as I walked in with two guns in my hands, everybody was laughing. I don't know what was so hilarious. I stopped and thought, "This is pretty funny. I am going to feel pretty stupid running around here with guns in my hand."

I put the guns back in the holsters and walked back toward my van, and there was the guy standing by Park Avenue, the one who wanted to hit me with a case of corn. "It's not worth it, cuz. It's really not worth it," he said.

I grabbed him by the neck and slammed him against the car door. The guy begged me for his life, fearing I would kill him. I turned, and I could see people in the coffee shop looking at me. I knew I looked foolish. I was running on Seven Mile Road near Woodward in Detroit with guns in my hand. I did look like an idiot. I just stopped fighting. Instead, I turned around, got in my car, and went home. My wife was out playing Bingo that night. News travels fast in the community. A lady approached her and told her she needed to go home because her husband was in trouble.

The Final Explosion

That next morning, as I was waking up for the day, Sue walked up to me and fell to her knees.

"Leave them alone," she begged me. "Please, leave them alone. They have families."

"How about us?" I said angrily. "Don't we have a family? Don't we have kids?"

LOCKED IN HATE

"It's okay," she said.

"You think it's okay, huh? One day when they kill me, will you think it's okay? No, it's not okay. I'm going to even this score no matter what. It's not okay."

I left the house that morning even more determined to kill them. Part of me didn't want to hurt them because of my wife, but I still wanted to kill them for myself. That's when I got a stolen truck. I filled it up with five barrels - 55 gallons of gasoline - and put 12 sticks of dynamite in it. I took a MAC-10 Uzi and three shells for backup. I hired my friend Johnny, a Vietnam veteran who knew how to make bombs. He made the base of the bombs. I finished them and added a timer and a detonator inside the tank to blow it up, and I purchased a 300-foot cable. Then I called Johnny.

"Johnny, I'm not going to let you get hurt on this job," I said. "I'm going to drive the truck, and when that truck hits the wall, all I want you to do is hit that one switch and this building is going to blow up like a hydrogen bomb. This way, they'll collect from their insurance, or they will not collect from their insurance, and everybody is going to go his way. If they collect, they're going to get big damages to the structure, and they won't get enough money. If it's too much damage, they may not collect, and they can build it, and everybody will go back home in peace."

It was Tuesday night—club night. Johnny and I went and hung out for a while. There was no way I was going to get busted. No way was I was going to do 20 years in prison. I had the truck hidden in the building close by, and I drove it that night. Once we got to the store, we saw cops in the Coney Island restaurant next door, which used to close at about 2 or 3 in the morning. I didn't want to get in a shootout with the police, so I told Johnny we would come back next Tuesday.

A week later, on a cold and snowy February night in 1988, I started my evening at the club to make an appearance. I left to pick up Johnny as planned, but he was not there. At a time without cell phones, I couldn't reach him. I decided not to wait for him. I have the body of an athlete. I figured that I was a fast runner and planned it all out in my head. I was going to wire the truck and set it off. I'd drive it into the building. It would give me three minutes to jump off. By the time I ran to my car, I'd be there in six minutes.

I drove the truck into this empty building. I didn't want to put off bombing the store another week. I was taking a risk having a stolen truck at this point, and having filled it with gasoline and dynamite, I knew I had to blow up the store that night. I opened the gas tanks, and the windows were closed. Fumes filled the truck. Consumed with rage, I wasn't thinking clearly. I wired everything up. I backed up the truck, and I tied the steering wheel handles. "Here I go, God. Here I go," I thought. "Let it happen. I'm tired of it all. I'm going to do it."

The minute I lit the fuse, the truck caught fire. I felt like I was in the middle of a furnace. I sat in the driver's seat, and the truck was in flames. The fumes from all the gasoline tanks were burning my face. I placed my hands over my eyes and cheeks to put out the fire. I dropped a big brick on the gas pedal, and the truck took off. I could hear the roar of the engine. I opened the door and jumped out. I heard the truck blowing up—one loud boom after another. I felt the vibration in the ground. The earth was shaking, but I couldn't see. The explosions blinded me.

I was now on fire. I rolled my body in the snow. I tried rubbing my eyes, but I couldn't see clearly. I saw blurry images, and I began running. I just kept thinking, "I need to see … I need to see."

I continued running down the street, but I couldn't feel anything but extreme heat. The adrenaline was pumping, and I ran until

I heard someone sounding a horn. "Jump in, jump in!" said a man's voice. "Tom, it's me, Johnny."

He looked at me, and I heard him scream. "Oh, my God!"

"Oh, my God, what?" I asked.

"You don't know how bad you look."

"How bad do I look?"

"Pretty bad, Tom. Pretty bad."

"Okay, I know this lady down the street. She's a good customer of mine. Drive me there."

It was about 4:30 in the morning, and he drove me to Mary's house. She was a customer I became friends with, and she lived close by. I rang the doorbell. "Who is it?" Mary asked.

"Tom Naemi."

She recognized my voice and opened the door, and she began to scream. "Oh, my God!" She slammed the door.

"Open the door!" I shouted.

"You're such a mess! What happened to you?"

"Please, relax. You got some iodine, some alcohol?"

"Yeah."

She started screaming again. I shouted, "Calm down!" Her daughter brought me a bottle of alcohol and iodine. I touched my head and felt a lump, and I realized my skin had been melting. Lumps of skin were falling off my body. "Oh boy, I'm in bad shape."

I looked in the mirror, and it was horrible. I called Hani. I also called this girl named Lisa. She used to work for me. I asked her where somebody who got hurt should go. She said, "You jerk. You hurt yourself, didn't you?"

"No, no, no. One of my friends is hurt. Where should he go?"

"What kind of hurt?"

"He got burned."

"University of Michigan," she said. "Go to U of M Hospital."

I called Hani again. "Hurry up!" I told him. "Get over here and bring me a blanket."

When Hani arrived, he helped me take off my clothes and put them in a garbage bag, which he handed to Mary. "Listen, these go in the garbage," he said to her. "Nobody needs to see these clothes."

She began screaming yet again. I swear she was having a nervous breakdown, and I started to not be able to understand her. She was Polish, with an accent. Hani drove me to the hospital. While in route, I put my hands out the window to cool them off. My bones were sticking out, and my entire body was scorching. My head was melting, and my ears were crisp. I'll never forget the face of this guy when I walked into the emergency room. He started to scream: "Oh, my God! Don't move! Don't move!"

He later went to court to testify in my case. He testified that I was burned so badly that he had never seen anybody walk in that condition before. Most people would have been on the stretcher, dead—he told the judge. He said something like, "I see this guy walking on his own, wrapped in a blanket," he testified. "I said, 'No way on earth can he be alive.'"

LOCKED IN HATE

The three women who helped me that night followed Hani and me to the hospital. At the hospital, a nurse placed me in a giant tub of water. It was supposed to be cold, but as soon as I was dropped in, I could hear my body sizzle like steak on a grill. I felt like I was being barbecued. Then they got the giant tweezers, about the size of my arm. They started clipping at the skin on my face. Nurses then clipped skin off my body; I was bleeding like a hog that had been skinned. They kept cutting and cutting until I eventually passed out from the pain.

A Reflection on the Prison Cell of Hate

I didn't know Scripture at the time. I never knew God spoke to us about revenge and said, "Vengeance is mine" (Romans 12). My unadulterated hatred toward my competitors drove me to seek payback for what I perceived as injustice.

I was just like so many stories you read in the news about some idiot who shot someone or killed someone because he or she was mad about something. Human hatred can drive us to do things we would never imagine in a state of love. In the Book of Genesis, we read about Joseph's brothers having such hate for him. "When his brothers saw that their father loved him more than all his brothers, they began to hate him, and they could not speak peaceably to him" (Genesis 37:4).

Joseph also had dreams he shared with his brothers about being bowed to, and this infuriated the brothers even more, as they thought Joseph wanted to be their king. Their hate for Joseph was rooted in jealousy, and it drove them to sell Joseph to the Ishmaelites for 20 pieces of silver. They tricked their father into believing Joseph was savagely killed by an animal.

I was no different from one of Joseph's brothers. My own hatred for my competitors drove me to do despicable things. Has hate-driven you to do something you regret or know in your heart is wrong? Hate consumed me to the point of nearly killing myself trying to destroy someone else. Although I'm free from hostility today, many people are still locked in hate for one another. We love because God first loved us. "Whoever says, 'I love God,' but hates his brother is a liar. The one who does not love his brother whom he has seen cannot love the God whom he has not seen" (1 John 4:19-20).

I eventually turned to Scripture to deal with my anger and my hate. We can handle anger biblically by communicating to solve the problem. I spewed out hatred, verbally as well as physically. Ephesians tells us: "No foul language should come out of your mouths, but only such as is good for needed edification, that it may impart grace to those who hear" (Eph. 2:29-32).

People cannot read our minds. We must speak the truth in love. That is right; love is the virtue that helps us release ourselves from the prison of hate. It is not enough to love our family. Jesus calls us to love our enemies. "But I say to you, love your enemies and pray for those who persecute you" (Matt. 5:44).

I was malicious and out for revenge. Ephesians also teaches us that we are not to "grieve the Holy Spirit of God, with which you were sealed for the day of redemption. All bitterness, fury, anger, shouting, and reviling must be removed from you, along with all malice" (Eph. 4:30-32).

I was too consumed by hate that I could not "be kind to one another, compassionate, forgiving one another as God has forgiven you in Christ" (Eph. 4:32). In Ephesians, we are encouraged to stay

LOCKED IN HATE

current. We must not allow what is bothering us to build up until we lose control. It is important to deal with what is bothering us before it reaches critical mass. This is exactly what I didn't do. I allowed years of anger to build up, and then I would have moments when I exploded with such deep hate in my heart. I never dealt with the root cause of my anger or sought personal peace.

What I never did was attack the problem; instead, I attacked the people. Along this line, we must remember the importance of keeping the volume of our voices low. Proverbs tells us not only does what we say make a difference but how we say it. If we are coming from a place of hate, we are going to express our words with that same hostility. What I should have hated was evil itself. Instead, I was driven by it. I was harboring hate and not relying on God to help me release the hatred within.

We need to focus on the virtue of love. There are many ways to show love to thy enemy. You can start by praying for them as our Lord has instructed us to do. Lift them up in prayer. As Catholics, we can recite a Rosary for them or lift them up when we receive the Body and Blood of Christ at Mass. We can confess our hatred for them in reconciliation. It's easy to love your friends and family. The true test is loving those who hurt you.

Do you find yourself in these scenarios that could cause hate?

- Someone stabbed you in the back
- Someone lied about you
- Someone hurt a family member
- You have witnessed or experienced injustice
- Someone stole from you

FREEDOM BEHIND BARS

Reflective Questions:

These are the questions we could ask ourselves if we are locked in the prison of hate.

- Who are my enemies?
- Why do I hate them?
- Where does the hate truly stem from?
- What can I do today to express love for them?
- How can I start to heal from the hate for them?

If you are locked in hate, here are some more Bible verses to reflect on:

Do not leave room for the devil. The thief must no longer steal, but rather labor, doing honest work with his own hands, so that he may have something to share with one in need (Ephesians 4:27).

If we claim to have fellowship with Him and yet walk in the darkness, we lie and do not live out the truth (1 John 1:6).

If we love our Christian brothers and sisters, it proves that we have passed from death to life. But a person who has no love is still dead. Anyone who hates another brother or sister is really a murderer at heart. And you know that murderers don't have eternal life within them (1 John 3:14-15).

Chapter 3

LOCKED IN FEAR

Finding Freedom in the Virtue of Faith

"Seek me and you shall find me for I have great plans for you, not plans of woe but plans of good things; plans of salvation" -Jeremiah 29:11-13.

±

Michel de Montaigne was known as an influential writer and philosopher during the late French Renaissance. Five hundred years ago, Montaigne said: "My life has been filled with terrible misfortune; most of which never happened."

Worry can consume our lives and cause us to make very bad decisions based on fear—fear of what might or might not happen. I was locked in fear for many years. It has been reported that most of what we worry about never really happens.

Since being released from prison, I have given my testimony to thousands of people—standing at a podium, in churches, or sitting across the table one-on-one. I've shared my story with many audiences, but it's the reporters and talk show hosts with their prodding questions who bring back the most painful memories.

"What about your wife and children?" reporters have asked me.

"What about them?" I would often respond.

I don't like to think about that part of my past—my family. I really don't like to talk about it. I remember telling parts of my story vividly, both during an interview and during a talk where I delivered my testimony. It's still so difficult for me to put the pain into words.

This time speaking at Sacred Heart Seminary in Detroit, I was discussing how God calls us even when we don't realize we have been called. I was explaining the part of my story when I was in the hospital, wrapped up like a mummy from head to toe. On one particular day, my friend Zak visited me. I couldn't open my eyes, but I heard the horror in his voice.

My left hand was so badly burned that doctors had to put it in a cast. They tied it very tightly so the skin wouldn't rip off and further damage the hand. I remember Zak coming in, and I couldn't see. "Tom, are you blind?" Zak asked. "Can you hear me?"

"Yeah, I can hear you.'"

Using my free hand, I tried to open my eyelids to look at Zak. I could see him crying.

"I am alright, man," I said. "Don't worry about me."

We sat talking for a while, but I don't really remember the conversation.

The Beginning of the End

While in the hospital, the police came several times to question me. I was telling this part of my testimony to a reporter one day. I remember this one particular conversation with a reporter, and I got sidetracked again.

FREEDOM BEHIND BARS

"What about your wife?' she asked.

"My wife?" I asked.

I couldn't help but cry. I tried to maintain my composure, but I couldn't. My wife was a good woman. I could recall seeing her face in the hospital and realized that is my biggest and only real regret that I caused her and my kids so much pain.

I have always said that I don't regret going to jail because that is where I met Jesus. People ask me that all the time: What do I regret? My regret is only the pain I caused others. I don't regret being put behind bars. Behind bars is where I was set free. It is the greatest thing that could ever happen to any man on Earth, after all—to find Christ. It didn't matter that it took being locked up for Him to find me. It only matters that I was finally free. But I regret what happened because my family paid the heavy price.

I had dozens of friends and family come from all over to see me in the hospital—hundreds of them, actually. I had so many people visit me that one day the head nurse named Gloria began to question me. "Who are you?" she asked.

"I'm Tom Naemi."

"Yeah, I know your name, but who are you?"

"I'm Tom Naemi. I don't understand your question."

"Yeah, I know you are Tom Naemi, but what is your position?"

"What position? I own a store."

"You know, I have been the head nurse for 25 years. I've never seen anybody get this many visitors in my life. Your family is banned from the visiting room."

"Okay, why is that?"

"Because you have 200 people coming every day. It is crazy."

It's not uncommon for people to travel by caravan to visit family or friends, so dozens of people a day visiting me was normal by Chaldean standards.

I stayed in the hospital for about three months, enduring surgery after surgery. The surgeries were for my hands, ear, and legs. They wrapped me up and stapled everything together. They took skin grafts from my stomach.

Doctors had to let my right ear hold together a little bit and get firm before they could operate on it. I remember that some of the skin grafts on my leg didn't hold. My right leg was so badly damaged they had to do another skin graft on it. For a burn patient, I didn't think I looked so bad, but I wanted to see for myself. I had been in the hospital for so long, yet I hadn't seen all the damage. When my brother Ned came to see me, I really wanted to look in the mirror.

"Give me a mirror, man. I want to see how I look," I told him.

"No, you don't need the mirror," Ned replied.

My voice grew louder. "Give me a mirror!"

Ned was trying to spare me the pain. It was just weeks earlier when I had tried to jump out the second-floor window shortly after getting to the hospital, before all the surgeries. I was like, "I'm not going to live like an ogre and have people make fun of me. I'd rather die; it'd be easier."

Hospital nurses stopped me. They tied my hands to the bed to prevent me from committing suicide. I remember when they took the bandages off. I felt like the ugliest human being you'd ever seen—no nose, no lips, no eyelashes. I thought about the movie about the final 12 hours in the life of Jesus, where the woman plays Satan. She looked a lot prettier than I did.

I remember having surgeries. They put a plastic cup on my ear to hold it together, and they stapled it. My brother never did give me the mirror that day, but I eventually did see my grotesque self, weeks later.

When my kids came, it was especially tough. My kids were so scared—terrified to see me. They didn't get near me. My daughter recognized my voice, but she would not come closer than 5 feet from me. She was only 4 years old at the time. The life I knew was changing forever. Although I was not sure of what would happen next, I knew my life as a husband and father ended when the bomb exploded.

While in the hospital bed one day thinking about my life, the police came and pounded me with questions. "Do you remember this person?"

"Remember who? What? I don't even know what you're talking about, officers."

"How'd you get burned?"

"In a car."

"How?" the officer asked.

"Fixing an old car."

I pressured my mechanic the night of the explosion to go to cousin George's house and burn an old car. It was my plan to tell the police and others how I got burned. The story was that we were trying

LOCKED IN FEAR

to start a 1977 Mercury my cousin George bought. Poor George—he got a year of prison for lying in my case. The mechanic blew up the carburetor to make it look like I was burned by the car while fixing it. We filed an Oak Park police report, and I told the police I was taken from Oak Park to the hospital. The mechanic didn't get in trouble, but George was charged for filing a false police report, and he wouldn't testify against me. He's the only one who had an old car. I couldn't think of anybody else. I think he forgave me. At least, I hope he did. I love George. He's a good man.

A Premonition

One night while still in the hospital, I fell into a deep sleep. I dreamed I was on a drive longer than five hours and came across a monastery on top of a mountain. It was called Shaikh Metah (Aramaic for "St. Matthew"). I went in and prayed. While there, I heard a man speaking very loudly, "Everyone who comes in must take off your shoes. This is holy ground."

While inside, I saw the pile of shoes outside. However, I was afraid to take off my shoes because I was wearing an expensive pair. I did anyway. I prayed. I remembered having a feeling of great peace. In the dream, I left that place and drove a couple more hours to Alqosh, a town in the north of Iraq. When I arrived, I was greeted by cousins. I also met a priest at another monastery.

"Father, what are you doing here?" I asked.

"What do you mean? I am always here. Let me show you my monastery," the priest replied.

With a twinkle in his eyes, he showed me around. "Let me show you something," he said.

FREEDOM BEHIND BARS

The priest had a collection of old guns downstairs that were collecting dust. Then I saw this beautiful old Bible; it had gold-rimmed thick paper. The paper felt like velvet. I dusted it off and opened it. I thought, "How on Earth could they leave this Bible here just collecting dust?" I was mesmerized by it. "Come on in and let me show you the church," said the priest.

We walked back upstairs, down a dark hallway, and toward 10-foot-high black doors. I opened them and saw a wall with beautiful images. I saw pictures of Christ. I felt such peace at that moment. I felt at home. Suddenly, I heard two women talking. I soon realized they were voices in my hospital room. I slowly opened my eyes. There, standing in front of me, were my sister Hanna and her friend Sue.

After they chatted a bit, I told them about my dream. At first, I had no idea what it meant and didn't really think much of it at the time, and I didn't know it was a premonition of what was to come. Hanna and Sue visited me about a month before I was released from the hospital. I was finally recovering from the bombing incident; I lost about 40 pounds but was still gaining my strength back. The food was awful! They stayed for a bit and chatted about nothing, really. I don't remember the conversation other than them asking me how I was doing. They didn't ask me if I really did try to blow up my competitor's store.

After about three months in the hospital, I was released. It was May 1988. Shortly after returning home, I received calls from the banks; they were calling off my banknotes. All my bank accounts were frozen. I couldn't get a loan from anyone. The food supplier I did business with and the bank tried to take my store. I knew then that

LOCKED IN FEAR

there was no such thing as normal for me anymore. Fear had taken a strong hold over me, and it changed the course of my life.

Reflection on the prison cell of fear

Fear and doubt are the enemies of the faith. The words "Be not afraid" are found throughout the Bible. Fear can be destructive. I have talked to so many people who are suffering from depression and anxiety, and many of them are youth. Fear can play a significant role in those cases. Fear holds people back and causes thoughts of doubt.

Since being released, I have prayed over countless people and often end up talking to them about their lives. I hear talk of fear so often. So many phrases have included:

"I can't do it."

"I am a failure."

"I am not smart enough."

"I can't pass the college test."

"I don't fit in."

"I am not pretty enough."

The lies of the devil create fear in our hearts. I come across young men afraid to commit to a marriage out of fear of thinking they don't have enough to offer. God tells the apostles not to be afraid. In this reading of the Book of Matthew, the apostles thought Jesus was a ghost. It was about walking on water. As long as Peter was focused on Jesus, Peter was not afraid and walked on water, but as soon as Peter focused on the water, he panicked; his mind was analyzing that man can't walk on water. Fear and doubt took over, and Jesus had to save Peter from drowning (Matt. 14:22-33).

FREEDOM BEHIND BARS

There is a healthy fear, and that fear is reverence for God; it means to not use God's name in vain and to keep the Sabbath holy and live a holy life. Some people are not just locked in fear; they are being choked by it. The nation saw this after the presidential election in 2016 when Donald Trump was elected the country's 45th president. Many of those who didn't vote for him reacted with anger stemming ultimately from fear. Granted, campaigns themselves often prompt fear in people, and so does the media coverage of his campaign. But should we allow fear to render us unable to function on a daily basis?

Following the election, some college students could not cope. Around the country, it was reported that some were so upset that professors canceled midterms. Other colleges set up rooms for students to play with Play-Doh and coloring books. The media reported how there was an increase in guns purchased, and on social media, the opponents called the election an injustice. Hollywood celebrities threatened to move out of the country if Trump won, yet none packed their bags.

Is the reaction just fear?

Next term, we ended up with Joe Biden as the president and that election came with a new set of fears for a whole lot of people. I feared for my future and my financial stability so much that I firebombed my competitor's store, almost killing myself in the process. I was not only suffocating from the fear; I was dying from it. How do you cope with fear? It's possible through faith in Christ. Scripture does not just merely mention fear, but it addresses it often enough that it has been claimed there is a verse on fear for every day of the year.

The Bible is full of truths related to issues such as fear that leads to anxiety. As Christians, God gives us authority to use these

LOCKED IN FEAR

truths as weapons to combat whatever we experience or feel that doesn't agree with His Word (Ephesians 6:17).

There are several powerful Scripture truths about anxiety and fear. You should not only read these verses but get in the habit of speaking these Scriptures with sincerity. It could help build your faith and defeat your worries.

When it came to business and success, what I failed to realize is what Jesus said to us in the Gospel of Matthew: "Therefore, do not be anxious, saying, 'What shall we eat?' or 'What shall we drink?' or 'What shall we wear?' For the Gentiles seek after all these things, and your heavenly Father knows that you need them all. But seek first the kingdom of God and his righteousness, and all these things will be added to you" (Matt. 6:31-33).

Also, in Matthew, we read, "You need not worry about anything. Instead, seek first the kingdom of God and His righteousness and trust that all of your needs will be met."

My rage not only stemmed from fear but also from ego. I didn't know the importance of the words, "Humble yourselves, therefore, under the mighty hand of God so that at the proper time He may exalt you, casting all your anxieties on Him, because He cares for you" (1 Peter 5:6). We are called to humble ourselves before God and trust that He will promote us at the right time. We are called to cast all of our worries, fears, and anxieties on Him because He cares for us and will ultimately lead us to where He wants us to go.

When things are out of our control and fear sets in, which was evident after the presidential elections and during the COVID-19 Pandemic, as Christians, we are called to pray. "Do not be anxious about anything, but in everything by prayer and supplication with thanksgiving let your requests be made known to God. And the

FREEDOM BEHIND BARS

peace of God, which surpasses all understanding, will guard your hearts and your minds in Christ Jesus" (Philippians 4:6–7).

I am not saying the virus isn't reason to be concerned or that certain people in politics aren't detriment to our country. What I am saying, we can be proactive, not paralyzed by fear. We do what we can, but we must leave the rest to God, He permits things to happen. There is no need to be anxious about anything. Instead, make your request known to God through prayer and thanksgiving. The peace of God guards your heart and mind in ways that none of us can truly understand.

The dream I had prior to Hannah and Sue walking into my hospital room was a prelude to the peace I would ultimately find in Christ. Jesus said, "Peace I leave with you; my peace I give to you. Not as the world gives do I give to you. Let not your hearts be troubled, neither let them be afraid" (John 14:27). That story will come later.

We have the peace of Jesus, which is far better than what the world offers, and so our heart is not troubled or afraid. There is no fear in Jesus. Scripture also teaches: "For you did not receive the spirit of slavery to fall back into fear, but you have received the Spirit of adoption as sons, by whom we cry, 'Abba! Father!'" (Romans 8:15).

We have the Holy Spirit, and He has freed us from fear. We are not afraid of anything because we are protected and taken care of as a child of God. No matter who the president is in the United States, God is always in charge. Those who reacted with rage and fear may not realize this important Christian principle. That is why we always pray, "Let His will be done."

I faced death with my own hands. It was through Scripture I later learned that there is no fear in death when you have God. "Even though

LOCKED IN FEAR

I walk through the valley of the shadow of death, I will fear no evil, for you are with me; your rod and your staff, they comfort me" (Psalm 23:4).

Even when we are in dark valleys, we fear no evil because God is with us. His rod and staff comfort us. My fear of failure, losing business, and money ultimately led me to prison because I did not put my faith in God. "For God gave us a spirit not of fear but of power and love and self-control" (2 Timothy 1:7).

God has not given us a spirit of fear or shyness. Instead, we have power, love, and self-control. You will find none of these in fear but only in your faith for our Lord and Savior. In order to rid my mind of fear, I had to fill up my heart with love and faith. The virtue of faith in God that trust in Him combats the vice of fear. 1 John 4:18 reads, "There is no fear in love, but perfect love drives out fear because fear has to do with punishment, and so one who fears is not yet perfect in love."

Do you find yourself in these scenarios that cause you to be afraid?

1. Loss of a job
2. Family is fighting
3. Friends have abandoned me
4. I don't have an education or employable skills
5. There is so much political and corporate corruption in the country
6. There is so much unrest in the world
7. Politics and political divide destroying our country
8. A virus is going to kill my family or me

Reflective Questions

1. What are your greatest fears?
2. How do you typically cope with your fears today?
3. How could you bring Jesus into the equation to help you put

your fears in perspective?
4. How can you trust Jesus more today?
5. How can you surrender your life to Jesus today?

If you are locked in fear, here are more Scripture versus to meditate on:

For he has said, 'I will never leave you nor forsake you.' So, we can confidently say, 'The Lord is my helper; I will not fear; what can man do to me" (Hebrews 13:5b-6).

"For God gave us a spirit not of fear but of power and love and self-control" (2 Timothy 1:7).

"Even though I walk through the valley of the shadow of death, I will fear no evil, for you are with me; your rod and your staff, they comfort me" (Psalm 23:4).

Chapter 4

LOCKED IN LIES

Finding Freedom in the Virtue of Truth

"Whoever conceals his transgressions will not prosper,

but he who confesses and forsakes them will obtain mercy" -Proverbs 28:13,

±

I was in serious trouble.

I hired a well-known attorney; let's call him "Mr. Big Time." So, Mr. Big Time told me not to worry because the prosecutor didn't have real evidence against me; they didn't have a case to put together.

I remember telling this part of the story to friends at dinner one night. I give my testimony as soon as people get a glimpse of my story. As the years passed since being released from prison, I have shared my testimony with thousands of people. Whenever I am preaching or teaching, my personal experiences are weaved into the lesson.

I trusted Mr. Big Time. As the legal team began to prepare for court, I discovered that my case was assigned to a judge I didn't believe would give me a fair trial. She basically did whatever she wanted, according to my intel. So much of my story sounds like a

LOCKED IN LIES

conspiracy, but it is the life I lived, and it is supported by court documents, news reports, and people in my life.

Shortly after I was given the news about the judge, I was tipped off that so-called prominent people in the Chaldean community had the judge's ear and were telling her to find me guilty no matter what happened in court. Mr. Big Time assured me that the only way they could find me guilty was through my medical records, and by law, the prosecutors could not submit them in court without my consent, which I would never give.

I was so badly burned that the medical records would hurt me in court. It could help prove I blew up the car myself. The prosecutor tried to get my medical records admitted into the trial, but Mr. Big Time kept objecting. Somehow, the judge allowed it. I heard that a prominent businessman, someone very influential in the community, called her on behalf of my competitor and pressured her into allowing my medical records to be submitted. Is this the truth? I don't know for sure. I only know what I was told and, of course, what transpired in court. Months later, while sitting in prison, I would recall that day in court, which sealed my fate. The judge was sitting, the court was in session, and her words repeated in my head over and over again.

"I'm going to admit the evidence," I heard the judge saying.

My attorney stood up and quickly objected. "You can't, Your Honor. By law, you have no jurisdiction over it." The judge responded with something like, "I don't care. It's my courtroom. I'm going to do whatever I want. Take it to the court of appeals."

I knew that no matter what happened, I was going to do at least five years by the time my case reached the court of appeals. I also knew that the appeals court doesn't typically reverse what the lower court rules. The chances of the appellate court siding with me were slim.

At that moment, I planned my escape. I was going to Iraq. I didn't care that we were in the middle of the trial. I had no chance at that point. I knew once my medical records were admitted into court, I would be found guilty.

Stress overcame my entire being. I couldn't sleep; I stayed up all night watching my wife and kids sleep. Who would take care of them? The more I thought about it, escaping to Iraq seemed like the only solution. I didn't tell my wife at first. I didn't want to tell her. I didn't want to tell anybody, for that matter, but I needed help.

I called some friends and planned my escape in more detail. It wasn't that difficult since Michigan sits on the border of Canada. It was only a 30-minute drive from my home to the border. With the help of three friends, I not only devised an escape route but also what I would do once in Iraq. I had done some research and gotten some brochures about the slaughtering business. I planned to purchase equipment that could be shipped to Iraq. I was going to buy a slaughterhouse and sell beef. The meat was in high demand in Iraq. I already knew how to butcher and how to run a business. Breeding cattle couldn't be that difficult to figure out, I thought.

I didn't tell my wife until the day before I left. "You have money," I told her.

I figured she had enough money for about six months. "You can wait until the kids get out of school and then pack up and go live with your mom."

She looked at me and knew I was serious. All she said was, "Okay." I can still see that worried and sad look on her face. I left for

LOCKED IN LIES

Baghdad in August of 1988. As soon as I landed, news hit that the Iran-Iraq War had ended. I heard gunshots when I first landed, but shortly after, they ended. Everyone who greeted me upon my arrival called me a blessing. I was good luck; I came to Iraq, and the war ended.

Life was easy in Iraq at the time. People worked a few hours a day and worked hard. It would get extremely hot during the day, with temperatures topping out at 120 degrees. They have their Middle Eastern version of siestas in Iraq. Everyone took naps between 12 and 2 p.m., and by 3 in the afternoon, they would go back to work until about 8, 9, or 10 p.m. It depended on the business. Business owners had stores, bars, and the like, and they came home to spend time with family; they walked around the city when everyone finally closed for the night, around 10 p.m. It was a happy, simple life.

I stayed with my cousin, George's brother Shokhet in Baghdad. He had a big house, and I had my own room. It was like a suite. George was about to go to jail for a year because of me, and I was in Iraq living with his brother.

While in Baghdad, my business was approved by the government; I began working on the cattle ranch. I was able to purchase 200 acres of land for what was considered very cheap at the time. The Iraqi government-financed my project, almost 90 percent of it. They wanted the beef industry to grow. The government had money, and I was approved to get equipment shipped from Italy; I even got documents to say, so I could go freely in Iraq without getting harassed by anyone. That is how things worked in Iraq. Everything was controlled by the government. I didn't want some military guy or some government official bothering me. Even the government knew I needed papers to say, "leave this guy alone."

FREEDOM BEHIND BARS

While I worked on my business and everyone went on with their own business, a daily comment from the people was, "Praise God." Those were the words that came out of every Christian for days and weeks after the war. I heard this everywhere and every day from everybody. One afternoon, my cousin Shokhet asked if I wanted to take a drive up north. I figured a few days away might be nice, and the four of us headed out on the trip. My cousin Sabah was the driver and was afraid of driving on the highway with semi-trucks, so every time we passed a truck, he would swerve in and out of the lanes. I thought we were going to die. I begged him to pull over so I could take over.

He was such a bad driver that when we would go to the airport in Bagdad to pick up or drop off family who visited, he would always end up making a wrong turn right into Saddam Hussein's castle. It was a round-about turn, and Sabah would always take the second turn into his driveway. In seconds, the military with machine guns would be screaming in Arabic for us to stop and pointing their guns at us. "Khaff," they shouted. There were about a dozen guards. "KHAFF" means STOP in Arabic.

So, we stopped, and he would turn back around. He did that at least three times while I was there. He scared the heck out of me every time. As I sat in the driver's seat traveling north, I felt complete déjà vu. "I have been here before," I said.

"You couldn't have," said Shokhet. "These are new freeways. Saddam Hussein just put these in."

"I have been here," I repeated. "I have been on this drive. I know I have. There is a monastery about five and a half hours away."

"Okay, drive there, then," said Shokhet.

So, I did. I drove right to Shaikh Metah (St. Matthew's Monastery). There it was—the same monastery I had seen in my dream just months earlier while recovering in the hospital. It was at the top of the mountain. As I remember, it was in the shape of a large circle. Then we drove to a lower monastery in Alquosh.

I told my cousins, "Watch! There is going to be a priest who will greet us. We will also see domed rooms, guns, a dark hallway, and a room with hand-painted walls."

There, greeting us, was a short-statured, heavy-set priest. He welcomed us inside. He took me aside and showed me the domed rooms upstairs, and then he said, "Come see my old gun collection."

I was in awe. I couldn't believe my dream was unfolding before my eyes. We walked through a dark hallway and entered a room with intricate hand-painted walls. Yes, the priest showed me the guns. My cousin Sabah put his hands on the big black doors before we entered and said, "The mighty God who has shown you all this has a plan for you."

We opened those doors, and there inside was a beautiful church. I think I always loved God but never really knew it. It wasn't until my premonition came true that I realized that I did, in fact, have love for the Lord. My plan was to stay in Iraq for the rest of my life. I was about to rent a house. I even registered my kids in a foreign school in Bagdad near the airport. I received finance for my slaughterhouse. I met with the department of agriculture in Iraq. I was doing all I needed to do to build a new life in Iraq. With the financing, I had a plan to have 400 cattle. My plan to stay in my homeland lasted only nine months. I tried to convince my wife to join me in Iraq with the kids, but she couldn't -- she wouldn't.

I tried calling a few times to convince her but with no luck. "Tom, I can't come," she'd say. "I am afraid. I can't live in Iraq."

"Don't worry, honey," I told her. "Do whatever you want to do. I'll see you in a little while."

I had so many sleepless nights fighting demons in my mind. I was filled with hate. I woke up every morning drenched in sweat. I soon realized that I had to go back. I couldn't leave my wife stranded. So, I left everything I had been working on in Iraq and planned my travel back to the United States.

I first flew to Mexico. I called friends and started catching up on what was going on. I heard my good friend Rick had been bad-mouthing me. My cousin, who Ray drove me to Canada to escape to Iraq, filled me in on what was going on back home. He and three other friends dropped me off in Windsor when I fled to Iraq. They had told me that Rick, the same guy who said, "My brother, my brother, anything you want. You name it, and I'll give it to you," was now bad-mouthing me.

"Tom, whatever you want, we're here," Rick told me as I fled to Canada and eventually to the Middle East. "Do you need money? Ten, 20, 50 thousand—whatever you want."

"I don't want anything," I answered. Now, on my way back to the United States, I heard he had been talking about me.

I found out that Rick told my brother: "You know, your brother cost us; his stupidity cost us hundreds of thousands of dollars. He brought these people into that neighborhood. We were doing this big business. We used to make a million dollars a year, and our profits went down about $300,000 to half a million."

LOCKED IN LIES

They claimed I brought the competition into their neighborhood because I bought this store that was doing big numbers. They blamed me instead of blaming others. I told my brother, "Don't worry. One day, we'll meet up again. I got something for him."

I continued to get calls about Rick.

"Man, he is talking crap about you," one guy told me. "You remember your friend Rick, how he used to call you, 'My brother?' He's talking about you now."

"Yeah, it's okay," I said. "My brother called me and told me already. No problem. I got something for that two-faced jerk."

"What are you going to do?"

"Man, I got a long arm in Detroit. All I have to do is pick up the phone and call a couple of my boys. They'll kill him in his own store."

I talked a big game, but in reality, I had enough. Who knows if any of it was true or just lies to enrage me more? I had been locked in lies for so long. I began to wear down a bit. I decided I had enough with the violence. I wanted to see my wife and kids. I wanted to turn myself in. A friend recommended an attorney who used to be a Wayne County prosecutor and knew the circuit court system and the judge well.

I was tired of the lies. My lies led me to buy two guns and go into a coffee shop to kill at least five men, if not six. I can't remember exactly. It's been so long, and it really didn't matter at the time. I was ready to kill anyone and everyone who angered me.

So, I hired this attorney; let's call him "Mr. Sensible." He convinced me to return to the United States by telling me he could get me less than 10 years but probably closer to 5 years. I could do that.

FREEDOM BEHIND BARS

With a $25,000 retainer, Mr. Sensible got started on my defense. After I flew from Iraq to Mexico, I traveled by car from Mexico City to Tijuana. My journey began at the border in Detroit and took me to the California border; I was almost back in the states.

A Reflection on the Prison Cell of Lies

What are lies, and what is truth? I was locked inside my lies so I could stay free in the world.

As Christians, we know that truth is found in following Christ. Truth with a capital T comes from scripture. I know my story sounds crazy, but it's my story, and one I hope helps others find healing.

Are you locked in your own lies? Perhaps you stand looking in the mirror, lying to yourself about who you are and how you live your life, justifying your actions much like I did. Where will the lies take you? Where have they taken you? The lies took me to prison.

We see that God is the truth. Jesus said, "I am the way, the truth and the life" (John. 14:6). As we speak the truth, we become godly. It becomes edifying instead of what the devil does and causes destruction. So, who are we following when we lie and mislead others from the truth? When we lie once, we must lie twice to cover for our first lie and lie four times to cover our two lies; before you know it, we have lied with every word that is uttered. We have weaved a web of lies.

Our Lord stated that the devil is the father of lies. In the Gospel of John, we read that "You belong to your father the devil, and you willingly carry out your father's desires. He was a murderer from the beginning and does not stand in the truth, because there is no truth in him."

LOCKED IN LIES

When the devil tells a lie, he speaks in character because he is a liar and the father of lies. What characters are speaking to you, and what lies are they telling you? Some people live their entire life as one big lie. Who really knows what the truth was for me back then? Perhaps if I had never listened to the devil, I would never have tried to blow up my competitor's store. I wouldn't have lost my freedom, my wife, my children—my life.

When we mislead people, we cause harm to others, whether it's destroying human character or misleading others about work, finances, faith, and themselves—to make others think better of us.

Deceiving is to mislead others about us for gain, and this is very evil because it hurts others in many aspects and lying is deceptive. We don't want to set people on the wrong path. The truth hurts sometimes, but we all need to hear the truth.

The devil told Eve, "You certainly will not die if you eat of this fruit." Well, we know the truth in scripture. Adam and Eve did die spiritually and later died physically; that's how sin and death came into the world.

Why did Cain kill his brother, Abel? He believed the lies. He was told by the enemy that Almighty God favored his brother over him. This angered Cain into slaying Abel.

In Proverbs, it reads, "Every word of God is tested; he is a shield to those who take refuge in him. Add nothing to his words, lest he reprove you, and you be exposed as a deceiver. Two things I ask of you, deny them not to me before I die: Put falsehood and lying far from me, give me neither poverty nor riches" (Prov. 30:5-9).

As we become children of God in our baptism, we must act and put on Christ Jesus in every word and action every day and every moment. Now, when I lie about anything, I feel that I am in pain because I harmed the Holy Spirit that's within me.

In Colossians, it says, "But now you must put them all away: anger, fury, malice, slander, and obscene language out of your mouths. "Stop lying to one another, since you have taken off the old self with its practices and have put on the new self, which is being renewed, for knowledge, in the image of its creator" (Col.3:5-10).

So, let us live godly lives and always speak the truth to one another. That way, the image of Christ will be seen in us. As the Word says in Colossians, "Let your speech always be gracious, seasoned with salt, so that you know how you should respond" (Col. 4:6). This means that we are to speak good, wholesome words so that people want more of Christ and less of the world.

In Romans, it reads, "And not only this, but we also exult in our tribulations, knowing that tribulation brings about perseverance; and perseverance, proven character; and proven character, hope" (Romans. 5:3).

That is what I eventually did. My tribulations brought me to Christ, and that is where I found my hope. Only truth can set you free from the prison of lies. Jesus is the way, the TRUTH, and the life. If we follow Him, we seek truth, and we find it. I had to face my lies head-on and speak the truth in order to be released.

Do you find yourself in these scenarios that could cause you to lie?

- Someone caught you doing something wrong
- You feel your livelihood is threatened
- You need to protect your family or a loved one
- You are trying to justify a situation

LOCKED IN LIES

- You are trying to protect your freedom

Reflective Questions

1. What lies are you telling yourself to justify your life?
2. What lies do you tell others?
3. How can you start to speak the truth with every word you utter?
4. What is the truth?
5. How can the truth set you free?

If you are locked in lies, here are some more BIBLE verses to reflect on:

Do not lie to each other, since you have taken off your old self with its practices (Colossians 3:9).

Who is the liar? Whoever denies that Jesus is the Christ. Whoever denies the Father and the Son, this is the antichrist (1 John 2:22). You belong to your father the devil and you willingly carry out your father's desires. He was a murderer from the beginning and does not stand in truth, because there is no truth in him. When he tells a lie, he speaks in character, because he is a liar and the father of lies (John 8:44).

Chapter 5

LOCKED IN DESPERATION
Finding Freedom in the Virtue of Hope

"A fool gives full vent to his anger, but a wise man keeps himself under control" -Proverbs 29:11.

±

I was giving my testimony to a church group, explaining how I wanted so desperately to avoid prison. I was fighting for my freedom. This is the next part of my story.

My brother Ronnie came to pick me up from Tijuana in a van, and together with my wife and kids and his wife and kids, we drove to San Diego.

"Drive me anywhere away from Chaldeans," I told Ronnie.

He drove us to a motel about 50 miles north of the Rancho San Diego area—that is where most Chaldeans in California lived at the time. While we were checking in, I spotted my cousin Ned. I mean, what are the odds of that happening? You have better odds of getting hit by lightning or winning the lottery. We engaged in some banter.

"Tom, what are you doing here?" he asked. "Everybody says you're in Iraq."

"Yeah, I just got back. Today is the first day I'm back."

"What did you do? You know you're on the FBI's Most Wanted List? You have been on the news for days, man."

"Yeah, I know," I said as I walked away. But he continued talking.

"I got out on a personal bond," I lied, just to get him to stop asking me questions.

The FBI wanted me, and I just wanted to get to Detroit and turn myself in, but first, I wanted to see my mom. I mostly wanted to spend time with my wife and kids.

"I want to see Mama," I said to my brother. "She knows I am back from Iraq. Take me to Mom."

"Oh, okay, Akhoni (brother)," he said, and he gave me a hug.

"You know what? Let's not stay in the motel," I said. "It doesn't matter now. Ned will tell everyone, anyway, that I am back. Let's just go over to Mom's and stay with her." She lived less than an hour from the motel.

I walked into my mom's house, and she was visibly stressed. She was crying and rambling on, speaking the Chaldean language, Sourath. She wrapped her arms around me and squeezed me with all her strength.

"Don't worry, Mom, I got out on bond," I reassured her. "Everything is okay. Who's in town from Detroit, Mom?"

"All your friends ... Rick, Ray - all those guys you hang out with - that big group. They are all here on vacation."

Of course, I thought — Ned, whom I saw earlier at the motel, told the rest of the guys I was in San Diego and my mom's phone began to ring. They continued calling every 10 minutes for about an hour, asking my mom if they could speak to me. Finally, I grabbed the phone from her hand.

"Yeah, who is this?" I asked.

"Hey, Naemi, you back in town? Oh my God, Naemi, you are back? Man, we have missed you. You have to come to the hotel."

It was Ray, Rick's cousin.

"Yeah," was the only thing I felt like muttering.

All I could think about was that if anybody had a problem, my pistol would solve it for me, but I didn't want to do that. I wasn't afraid of anyone, but I really didn't want to get into it with these guys.

I ended the phone call abruptly. I continued my dinner with my mom. The phone kept on ringing, but I ignored it. Every time the phone rang, however, my anger grew. I felt the rage boiling inside. I wanted to kill someone, but I continued talking to my mom as if nothing was going on.

"Why don't you answer the phone?" my mom asked.

"Mom, these guys talk bad about me, and I don't want to go because I don't want to hurt them," I said. "The last thing I want is another problem."

"Broni (my son), don't go."

"I'm not going, Mom. Don't worry," I said as I walked to get a glass of water. I sat back down, and the phone kept ringing. They must have called about 15 more times. I couldn't take it.

"Give me the phone, Mom," I shouted. She answered it and then handed it over to me.

"Hi, Tom," one of the guys said. "How have you been?"

"Fine," I muttered.

"Hello, brother, how are you? Come on over and hang out with us," another friend said on the line.

"I'm over at my mom's house; just got home."

"Come on over."

"Where you at?" I asked.

"I'm at a motel," one of the guys said as he named everyone with him.

I hung up, looked over at Ronnie, and signaled for us to leave.

"Don't go, Tom," my mom begged.

"Don't worry, Mom," I replied. "We are just going for a ride."

I walked over to Ronnie and whispered, "Come on, drive me to this motel."

When I walked into the motel room, I counted about eight guys. Rick was the first to stand up and shake my hand.

"Sorry, buddy, you're not man enough to shake my hand," I said.

"What?" he asked, clearly irritated.

LOCKED IN DESPERATION

"You're not man enough to shake my hand," I repeated.

"What is that supposed to mean?"

"You know exactly what I mean."

"Who do you think you are talking to?" he yelled.

"I'm talking to you!" He stepped closer to me, and there we stood, face to face.

"Rick, you sure as hell are not man enough to get in my face. You don't know what I'm capable of doing."

At that moment, all I could think about was my deep desire to butcher Rick. As I stood staring him down, the rest of the men stood up and pushed their way between us.

"What's wrong with you guys?" asked Ray. "Come on, sit down. You guys are brothers."

"No, we *used* to be brothers," I said. "We're not brothers anymore. We were brothers when everything was okay for Rick, but not when I went to Iraq; as soon as I left, this guy who calls me 'brother' started talking smack about me."

Rick responded, "No, no, I never said anything."

"Oh, now you're adding insult to injury," I shouted. "My brother is a liar? Bobby is a liar? This guy is a liar?"

Despite my rage-filled demeanor, I never drank. Everyone who knew me knew I was never seen with a beer or cocktail in hand. They knew this, yet they asked me if I wanted a drink. I knew something wasn't right. It was never clear to me why they would even ask me to drink.

One of the guys in the room poured me a glass of Johnny Walker Black on the rocks. I took the glass and drank the entire thing in one swig. I could hear the guys talking about nothing in particular. Three or four of them left so that there were about five of us men still in the room.

"Hey, Rick," I called out.

"What?"

"You're still not man enough."

"You know what I'll do?" asked Rick. "I will bust you."

"You know what, Rick?"

"What?"

"I am going to hit you so hard that by the time you raise your hand, you will be face down. You will be seeing stars. I've done it a million times, and one more won't be anything. You'll be just one more guy to add to my list."

"You know who I am?" he asked.

"Listen, Rick," I said calmly. "I know who you are. You beat up and slapped the crap out of a couple of punks. Who did you really beat up that was a real tough guy? Tell me one name."

"Alright, are you trying to check my character?" he asked.

"I know your character is garbage," I replied.

Rick stood up and walked toward me, and I started with one expletive after another. The other guys jumped in between us.

"Tom, let it go, man," said Ray.

"I just tell it like it is. I can't help it," I said.

Rick stepped right toward my face and began cursing, and with one punch, he hit me. I stood there and stared at him.

"Didn't I tell you? Didn't I?" I shouted.

With all the rage that I could muster, I swung with my clenched fist right into Rick's face. The force was so brutal that Rick's forehead went down and hit the table.

I hit him a second time. I could hear the busting of his nose. The bone came out. Blood rushed out and spilled out everywhere. I was now in full rage, and nothing was going to stop me. I hit him a third time in the jaw—*boom!*

With that third blow, Rick slumped over the table. I wanted to hit him again. I wanted to put a foot in his face, but Rick was out cold. After a few minutes, Rick managed to pull himself up and positioned himself to hit me, but I was quicker and jumped up to spin-kick him in the face. The kick ended up landing on his chest.

Rick was out again. The other guys stood up to rush to his aid. I slapped Rick's face to wake him up. Abe, one of the guys in the room, was built like a linebacker and tried to push me away from Rick, but I punched him in the stomach, and then I slapped Rick again.

"Hey, tough guy, wake up!" I yelled. I wanted to beat him up some more.

Rick tried to shake it off. He was barely moving.

"Come on, tough guy, let me show you what it's like to be a real man," I shouted even louder. Slowly, Rick was coming out of it.

"Didn't I tell you? You have to be a real man." I shouted again and hit him with such force I really thought I was going to kill him.

All of the men stood up and came after me. I could not stop hitting; I just kept punching. I was a mad man completely out of control. I hit Rick in the midsection. Barely able to stand himself, I took a swing at Ray. I felt his fist weaken and tighten. I was about to swing one more punch when I heard a man scream.

"No, no, this is Ray!" I turned around, and I couldn't stop myself. My fist was already in action. I swung on the other side and missed him. Ray grabbed me, and started pleading with me. "Please, Tom, stop," he begged.

"Okay, Ray, for you, I'll leave him alone. Otherwise, I'll kill him here. I'll bury him here. But for you, I'll leave him alone." Having trained in martial arts, I always glance at my surroundings in every situation. I also wrestled in high school. Not only did I have rage inside, but I was also trained to fight. I scanned every inch of that motel room, and I noticed something in Rick's hand. Just before that, I was ready to walk out. I had turned to Zeke and said, "Zeke, come on. You're going to drive me home."

I didn't have a car, and I had already told my brother to go home. I didn't want him to be a target of the police or be harmed in any way. As I got ready to leave, I watched every guy I could from every angle, including from the corner of my eyes. I could see that Rick had picked up a bottle of Rémy Martin. I positioned myself to swing-kick the bottle out of Rick's hand and then punched him in the face.

"Okay, Rick, if you're man enough to use that bottle, I will have to kill you right here and right now," I threatened. "It is your choice. If your hand goes up, I'm going to bury you right here. So, it's up to you. Make the choice."

I was standing with most of my back turned toward Rick.

LOCKED IN DESPERATION

From the side, I could see that Rick was bleeding. "I know you're bleeding pretty bad," I said. "You got away with it cheap. I was going to kill you, but the boys stopped me."

Rick stood with his head down, holding the bottle in his hand. I could tell he was thinking about what to do. "Okay, you're not man enough to use that bottle, huh? You're a coward. Cowards always talk behind people's backs." I really wanted Rick to try to swing that bottle at me. I just wanted an excuse to take him out. Rick put down the bottle on the table. It was over. "Come on, Zeke, you're driving me home," I said again as I began to walk out the door.

As soon as I walked into the house, I told my mom I had to go. I knew the FBI would be on the way. With everything else I was wanted for; I could now add nearly beating a man to death in a motel room in front of witnesses to the list. I knew Rick would end up in the hospital. I knew a police report would be made. I knew that one of those guys would call the FBI. They all knew I was a wanted man. The phone rang and on the other line was a man who had heard about the fight. I was barely back at my mom's house, 30 minutes max, and the word was out. I knew that it was just a matter of time before the feds would be at my mom's front door.

More calls came in. The word was out in the Chaldean community both in Detroit and San Diego about my full rage inside a motel room.

I started packing and called my brother Danny to pick me up. There was only one side street leading into my mom's subdivision. My other brother Dolor came in from the side street. Five minutes before he got there, a man rang the doorbell. I knew it was an FBI agent.

The man stood on the porch, knocking on the door and ringing the bell. I didn't run. I actually opened the door, knowing it would be an FBI agent. The agent stood about my size. He had on a white T-shirt and blue jeans. "Can I help you?" I asked.

I looked at him and searched for a gun. I just kept thinking, "This is an FBI agent, but he's stupid. I know he didn't come by himself, but I kept thinking that he's going down. I'm taking him down."

"Is there a Mr. Smith here?" he asked.

"No, sir. No, Mr. Smith here," I said.

"Do you know where he lives?"

I shouted to my mom across the room. "Mom, do you know where Mr. Smith lives?"

"No, son, I don't."

"Sorry, sir, we don't know where he lives," I said, staring into his eyes.

"Okay, thank you." He walked away. As he walked all the way to the end of the block, my brother pulled up, I put my bags in the trunk, and we left. As the agent walked back to his car, I headed to Mexico. Still, today I think about what the faces of the FBI agents must have been when they realized I was right in front of this guy's face, and I slipped right by. They must have been so angered.

Almost at the border with Tijuana, while riding in my Cadillac, my mom called me. This was when car phones, not cell phones, started to surface. My car phone cost me $2,500 back then.

I picked up the phone and didn't have the chance to say hello.

"Call the lawyer!" my mom screamed. "These agents are damaging the whole house.

LOCKED IN DESPERATION

They're pulling the cupboards, they're pulling the refrigerator, and they ripped all the screens. They came in from the back door, front door, every door."

"Don't worry, Mom," I assured her. "I'm almost at the border. Everything is going to be fine."

I crossed into Mexico and told my brother to go home. For some reason, I felt like I could speak Spanish. I don't know why, but I thought I picked up a fourth language just by entering Mexico. I remember telling this story while delivering my testimony, and I always laugh. It's so absurd to me. Why did I think I could speak Spanish?

Three Mexican men walked by me, and I started to try to speak Spanish. "Where's the Aeropuerto?"

"Down the street this way, then go that way," the men replied in English.

"Okay, thank you," I said.

I found a nearby payphone and dialed the police. "Give me the United States FBI," I told the operator on the other end of the line. Someone at the Bureau answered. "This is Naemi. You guys just raided my mama's house, and I'm wanted, but I want you to know there's nothing to panic about. I'm already in Mexico, and I'm going to meet you. I'm going to show up in court when the time comes."

"What, sir?"

"Listen, you can trace this call. My name is Naemi. I'm wanted by the FBI, but you don't have to worry. Nobody is going to get hurt. I'm going to leave the line open, so you can trace the call and know that nobody's life is in danger. I know you got a phone call, but don't worry, nothing is going to happen. I'm going to turn myself in Detroit."

FREEDOM BEHIND BARS

I left the phone hanging and headed to the airport. I got on the plane with a one-way ticket back to Iraq. Meanwhile, my wife and kids were still in California. It was worth the $4,000 I spent back then to get to Iraq. I stayed six more months there.

I eventually called "Mr. Sensible," and, knowing I was in good hands with this attorney, I decided to return to the U.S. My attorney assured me I would get less than eight years. "Okay, I think we got it—maybe five to eight years," he told me over the phone.

Not quite ready to face the judge, I decided to head to Canada. I thought I could pick up work and start a new life just across the border. While living there, I met a Turkish man who was a taxi driver. We became good friends. I spent time each day touring with him around Windsor. He eventually began to ask me questions.

"Why are you here?"

"I'm looking for a job," I answered.

"You know what, Tom? Not too many Americans come to live here. It's going to look really suspicious seeing you here. Is something wrong?"

"Yeah, I left my wife and kids, and I just don't want to live in America anymore."

"Go back home. That is no life. Go back to your family. Face your problems," he said.

Meanwhile, I was waiting for my attorney to tell me to come back and confirm I would get a less than an eight-year sentence. Nothing happened for a while, and I got tired of Canada. I eventually called another friend who picked me up in Windsor and drove me back into

LOCKED IN DESPERATION

Michigan to a cottage on Cass Lake in Keego Harbor. My friends visited me often. We used to make Masgouf, a Chaldean fish dish. It was my favorite. You never got Masgouf in prison. Three months into my cottage stay, Mr. Sensible called. "Let's do it," I said, and within days we headed to court.

The judge addressed me immediately. I am not going off of court records here, but off of my memory. She said something along these lines:

"Mr. Naemi, I never thought the day would come when you would appear before me. I can't believe you're here. Why did you run?"

"Well, you know, they tried to kill me, and I had to do something; I couldn't just sit around," I said.

"But you should have come to me," she replied.

"Yeah, I handled things the wrong way."

"Okay, you guys go have lunch," she said.

She was nice and cordial, I remembered. Her demeanor had me believing that my sentence would be what I expected—what my lawyer and I had talked about during those last few weeks.

We ate lunch in Greektown—my attorney and I, and about 10 friends. Something happened during lunch. I later heard that the judge was called. I never knew by whom, but I always had my suspicions. It really doesn't matter now, but I truly believe that man sealed my fate. The person who called her while we were on recess made her believe I was a major threat to society, so I was later told. After lunch, the judge was not so nice. Everything turned around. She took no time before she blurted out, "The 60- to 90-year sentence still stands. Take this man into custody right now."

FREEDOM BEHIND BARS

And, with a swift pounding of her gavel, life as I knew it was over.

There were rumors of groups of people in the community who had it in for me and knew the judge. So, I believe that some people in the community who got caught selling stolen goods cut deals with the feds, and they ratted others out. I was led away in chains. It was May of 1990, and I was heading to Jackson Prison in the State of Michigan. I was facing a life behind bars.

I walked into Jackson with 13 other men that day. This one guy must have been 6'5" and looked at me, scared to death. I called him Dan the Drug Dealer. "Man, I'm really scared," Dan said.

"Don't be scared," I replied.

"Why? How can you say that man?"

"Anybody messes with you, I give you my word, I'll cut off his head and put it where the sun doesn't shine."

He was the first but not the last one in prison to look at me like I was crazy. "What? You're nothing but a little guy," he said.

A Reflection on being locked in desperation

I have never really told my entire testimony. I think a lot of it has been suppressed because of the pain of it all, but occasionally, memories sneak up on me. Even while writing this book, I kept remembering things I hadn't thought about in years. The pain is too great when I start talking about my wife and kids. I never even told them my whole story. Maybe now they will know.

I went from being desperate to stay out of prison to desperate to get out. You do crazy things when you are desperate. Since I had a rage inside already, every other negative emotion brought out my rage.

LOCKED IN DESPERATION

If you look up the word "rage" in the dictionary or do a quick Google search, you will read a description like angry, fury, violent anger, or a feeling of intense, violent, or growing anger. It could associate with the fight-or-flight response. Rage could be activated in response to an external cue, such as an event that impacts negatively on the person. The phrase "thrown into a fit of rage" expresses the immediate nature of rage that occurs before deliberation. If left unchecked, rage may lead to violence.

Makes sense to me. That *was* me. I think you are getting the picture. Maybe you have done something stupid or made a huge mistake out of desperation. There are countless stories in the news demonstrating that desperation contributed to a tragedy like murder, suicide, or a crime like robbing a bank or stealing a car. I am not trying to justify crime or diminish a tragedy, but somewhere in the person's psyche, the thing that drove him or her to do something tragic could be desperation.

I was a desperate man trying so hard to avoid prison. Nothing I did kept me out, and desperation didn't get me out. Only Christ did; it is hope in the Lord that will set us free from the bondage of desperation. We place our hope in Him, in the heart of Christ. That is the virtue that will combat our desperation; hope for any salvation can only be found in our Lord. Hope can be looked at as theological virtue in the Christian tradition. Hope is a combination of the desire for something and the expectation of receiving it. The virtue is hoping for Divine union and eternal happiness. While faith is a function of intellect, hope is an act of will. We must seek Him to know Him. It was through scripture and prayer that I found my way. It was hope in our Lord and Savior that saved me.

FREEDOM BEHIND BARS

Do you find yourself in these situations that could cause you to be desperate?

- You can't pay your bills
- You are about to lose a job or business
- Your spouse is going to leave you
- You are diagnosed with a serious illness or disease
- You feel like there is no way out

Reflective Questions

1. What are you desperate to do or not do?
2. What do you think will or will not happen if you don't get what you want?
3. How would you talk to Jesus about your desperation?
4. What do you hope for today?
5. What plans does Jesus have for you?

If you are locked in desperation, here are some scripture verses to meditate on.

I cry out to you, Lord, I say, you are my refuge, my portion in the land of the living (Psalms 142:6).

For in hope, we were saved. Now hope that sees for itself is not hope. For who hopes for what one sees (Romans 8:24).

For I know well the plans I have in mind for you says the Lord, plans for your welfare and not for woe so as to give you a future of hope (Jeremiah 29:11).

Chapter 6

LOCKED IN RESENTMENT
Finding Freedom in the Virtue of Fortitude

Why are you downcast? O my soul? Why so disturbed within me? Put your hope in God, for I will yet praise him, my Savior and my God
-Psalm 42:11.

±

Long before I walked inside the prison walls, and for the first few years while there, I was locked in resentment.

"I am not the healer, and I am not the evangelizer," I said to a crowd in Mar Addai Chaldean Catholic Church in Oak Park, Michigan. It was 2006, months after I was released from prison. It is God who heals, and it is our Lord who gives me the words to speak. Sometimes, I don't know what I am saying; words come out of my mouth, and I know it is the Holy Spirit working through me.

One of the first congregations I ever spoke to was Pastor Stephen Kallabat's parishioners from Mar Addai Church in Oak Park, Michigan. It was built to accommodate an influx of Christians from Iraq. I often explain to people that I died in prison. The Tom Naemi who was filled with rage, ready to kill anyone who angered him—

LOCKED IN RESENTMENT

that Tom eventually died in prison, but not before spending more than a decade fighting the demons inside and out. I was even more in rage and filled with resentment when locked behind bars. I have delivered my testimony hundreds of times with the same messages of being locked inside oneself. It was not the prison bars that encased my soul; it was all the negative emotions locked inside, including resentment.

Like in 2006, when I was first released from prison, I told another part of my testimony to attendees at St. George Chaldean Catholic Church in Shelby Township, Michigan, during the Eastern Catholic Re-Evangelization Center's (ECRC) annual Awake My Soul event in 2012.

Inside the church and standing at the pulpit, a thousand eyes looked back at me. I had them hooked. I could almost hear the talking in their heads: "Is this guy for real?"

During the first 10 years behind bars, I was deeply oppressed; I would explode. Everyone in prison knew I was out to destroy if anyone got in my way. I had deep urges to attack. I knew that some of that rage stemmed from having to leave behind my wife and kids. I resented that I was behind bars and my enemies were free.

While I was in prison, my wife eventually divorced me, and my children grew up without a dad. That reality deepened the resentment that I harbored. I was known in prison as a madman, and I liked it that way. I lived in prison inside my own soul, and my only outlet was to attack anyone inside the walls of the real prison I called home.

In 1990, I walked into Jackson Prison, 40 miles west of Detroit, with 13 other convicted men. I stayed at Jackson for 47 days in the processing center before I got transferred behind the wall. This

FREEDOM BEHIND BARS

area is another part of the prison. It was the section where "Lifers" were. That was everyone serving life without parole.

The process was to first screen the prisoners and join them together into groups, such as the lifers, the high security, and the low security. They didn't place lifers - those who are spending the rest of their lives in prison - with people who had lower sentences. I was sentenced to 60 to 90 years, so I was grouped with the lifers. I was assigned the sixth block, second floor, cell number 6.

Jackson was my home for more than three years. From the moment I walked into prison, everything I knew about being human was wiped away. As soon as the prisoners arrive, they are forced to undress until they are completely naked and are given prison clothes. You strip in front of everyone. While ripping off my clothes, I felt every ounce of my human dignity being stripped away from me. Here I was, a grown man of 34 years, and I was being yelled at to strip naked.

"Strip down!" I can still hear them screaming at us. "Take your clothes off!"

There we lined up, one guy after another, being given clothes through a window by a 300-pound, 6-foot-4-inch guy, who was a mean-looking jerk. He handed me stained and dirty pants with paint splattered all over them.

"Please, give me another pair of pants," I said. He handed me the same pants.

"I want some clean pants, dude."

He looked at me with his belly hanging out over the counter and said, "Get out of my face." I stepped closer to him.

LOCKED IN RESENTMENT

"Come here," I said. "I want to talk to you."

As soon as he got close enough, I grabbed his shirt and pulled him toward me. I had my leg on the wall holding me up, and I started screaming, "I am going to kick your a**, you mother******! Wait until I catch you!"

This sergeant ran up to us and started screaming at me. He was about 6'6" feet and all muscle.

"Hey, Naemi!" he yelled. "Hey, you!"

He started to grab me, but I was still yelling at the guy behind the window. I now had a strong grip on his belly.

"Just wait until I catch you outside these walls!" I said. "I am going to kill you."

He was my first target in prison. The first time I saw him in the yard, he was hiding behind 20 guys. Who wouldn't want to hide in that place? Jackson felt like a haunted place. I felt like I was transferred into a horror movie. The bricks were old and dark; the gates were creaky. It gave me a creepy feeling. I felt like dead bodies were going to come out of the walls.

During a visit from one of my cousins early on during my prison stay, he said he felt sick and just all-around bad walking in the place. Your teeth and body were actually grimier after brushing and showering. Rusty water that looked more like something coming out of a beer tap streamed out of the faucet and showers. It sure didn't smell like hops, though; it was nasty. I would shower, and my skin would bubble up. God only knows what was in that water.

FREEDOM BEHIND BARS

Jackson was six floors high with 85 cells per floor. I was now living with the most abnormal people anyone could ever meet. I was surrounded by murderers, robbers, rapists, and pedophiles—all kinds of people who have committed the most heinous crimes. And they all believed one thing—there was no hope of ever getting out. They preyed on one another.

It happened almost instinctively and much like high school, but in the scariest, darkest, and most evil high school you could imagine; they formed cliques inside the prison. People flocked to their own kind based on criminal and ethnic background. There were groups of skinheads, Muslims, blacks, faithful Christians, and the strong guys who could fight. The Muslims were broken down even further based on their own beliefs. It was not about religion, really.

It was about being in a gang. Of course, there were those weak, young, white boys who never seemed to have a chance of surviving in prison without becoming someone's sex slave. They were raped daily; many killed themselves. White boys, as we called them, couldn't fight. The protector would eventually become the predator. The prisoner would befriend the weakling for a couple of days, shower together, and play basketball. The guy would vow to take care of the boy. Then, after a few days, the weak kid became a sex slave to the other prisoner for protection. It was just sick.

Every single day in Jackson was a violent day. Men were not only raped but also beaten down. They took drugs. People were stabbed, cut, and killed. I have witnessed up to 30 people in one day injured. Big fights of 20 to 30 people would break out; kidneys were punctured, and people were wounded and taken to the hospital—and, yes, some died. I have seen it all. One day in Jackson, I saw a prisoner

LOCKED IN RESENTMENT

named Big Red cut another prisoner's neck. His blood squirted out everywhere. I am often asked how people got weapons in prison. We didn't get them in. We made them there.

The prisoners worked in the metal shop. The prison would hire a foreman from the outside, and the labor was done by the prisoners, who got paid chump change, like $20 to $30 a month. These prisoners worked with electric sanders. One guy could make a shank in five minutes and sell it for $10. Ten bucks is good money in prison. He could make a weapon from anything. You can break down one chair, get up to 20 weapons and make $200.

Preying on the weak

As soon as a new prisoner arrived, the predators waited to size him up. One day, this Latino guy came in. He looked like a woman. He had big breasts, long hair, and not much of a manhood. We all saw him in the shower. After he walked in, a riot broke out. I asked the guard what was going on, and he told me they had brought a girl into the prison.

"A girl?" I questioned. "What do you mean, they brought a girl here?"

"That's right, man," he said. "They brought a girl in here."

"The predators were giving him things, handing him toothpaste, food, anything. They wanted him," I said.

The prisoners showered together—40 men per shower and 40 per line, so that there were 80 men at one time in the shower. There was no privacy in prison. It was the first time I saw a man who really looked like a woman; it was the strangest thing to me. Every moment in the shower

FREEDOM BEHIND BARS

made me sick. One time, I walked in, and a group of men was making out and having sex. I couldn't take it. I ran them out. I started shouting: "I AM GOING TO KILL ALL Of YOU! GET OUT OF HERE!"

The prison was the pit of all pits. There was absolutely no sense of morality. You had no dignity. I spent most of my time trying to figure out how to survive—mentally, physically, and emotionally. The moment I woke up every day inside my cell, I started a routine as part of my survival. It ended up being my daily life for nearly 16 years. I ate peanut butter and honey sandwiches every morning with a cup of instant coffee. Maxwell House Instant Coffee was $2 a bag. I used 2 ounces a day. My family sent me money so I could buy my own food. Peanut butter cost about $2 a jar, and honey was about the same. Otherwise, the food in prison was disgusting. Yeah, it looked good on the menu - chili, hot dogs, vegetables - but it tasted like you already ate it and threw it up.

I stayed locked inside my cell with only a bed and a toilet for about 23 hours a day. We had one-man cells in Jackson. We slept most of the day. I did pushups daily in my cell, watched TV until I got bored with it, and read my books. They let us go to the chow hall three times a day and outside in the yard for an hour. Every moment I was locked inside the cell, my resentment grew. My body and soul were both imprisoned, and there was no hope of getting out. When I did get out to the yard or the chow hall, I knew that the second I walked in, if anyone thought I was weak, I could get attacked or even killed.

I beat people up all the time—I had to. I already had the reputation of being crazy from the first day when I went after Mr. 300-Pound Prison Guard giving out clothes through the window. I went crazy, threatening to kill the guys having sex in the shower, but that was not enough. You could never let your guard down.

Any opportunity I could punch someone, I would. One day, a prisoner accused me of owing another prisoner money. I didn't stop to respond. I clenched my fist and, with all my rage, swung my elbow right into the guy's face. "Listen, man, anyone messes with me, I am going to rip his head off," I told him. "Get your sh** straight."

When I saw him next, he said, "Hey, '6 Second,'" which stood for my cell block and floor number. I looked back.

"Hey, man, that was a big mistake," he said.

"Yeah, it better be a big mistake; otherwise, you're going to die," I said.

Word spread in prison not to mess with Naemi. It wasn't just about setting the tone. I was angry. I had rage buried so deep inside that anything set me off. There was no consistency with what caused me to have an outburst. Anything from inside the prison to the outside world caused me to blow my temper. In 1991, Iraq was at war. It was all over the news. I was in the shower one day with 80 other guys, and one of them kept talking about Iraq and how he wanted to kill everyone there.

"We are going to nuke them," the prisoner shouted.

With every comment, I felt the anger rising.

"Who is 'we?' You piece of crap," I shouted. Still in the shower, I rushed up to him and, without a thought, pounded my fist into his face. The guy fell to the floor, water and blood splattered, and I kept pounding on his naked body. I stood over him, just hoping to beat the life out of him.

FREEDOM BEHIND BARS

The other prisoners shouted for me to stop, screaming that the police were coming. If they hadn't stopped me, I would have killed him. With every prison I was transferred to, I made sure I pounded on a few guys to let everyone know they better leave me alone.

For the most part, the prison was torture, not because of the fights but because of the silence and solitude. The hours were long. Every minute was an hour. Every day was a month. I looked at the clock, and it never moved. I had never seen anything like it. Every year was endless.

Time stopped in prison. Men would wake up every morning crying and cursing God that they were alive to breathe another day inside this hell. In the sixth block, where I lived, there were about two to three suicides a year, according to my recollection. There were also many attempted suicides. Try to imagine being locked inside a cell 23 hours a day. I had one hour a day to be in the yard.

The days were torture. I felt hopeless and that my life had no purpose. Nothing made sense. You knew you were going to die there; you just didn't know when. That was how most of the prisoners felt. Once a lifer walked into prison, that was it. From that moment, that was his life.

Reminded of life on the outside

Even though time seemed to barely pass inside, life went on outside of prison. I called home as often as I could. One day, still in the early '90s, I called my brother Kelly, who was crying. It turned out my younger brother Hani was shot and killed inside his store.

I just sat there, shocked. I couldn't speak. I began to cry. My brother. My Akhoni. The guy who knew me better than most people was now dead. I walked backed to my cell, hoping I could make arrangements to attend the funeral. My cousin Al offered to post bond for a temporary leave. My family was willing to pay the officers to escort me as well. The fee was $1,500 for the escort. The prison facility agreed to allow a temporary release, but just prior to being taken to the funeral, the permission was rescinded. Angry and distraught, I wrote a letter about the incident and sent it to various Catholic newspapers. I remember being surprised when one paper actually published it.

My resentment grew. I resented everyone, including the prison system and the authorities, who denied me a chance to mourn for my brother with my family. Instead, I remained inside the dark walls thinking about how Hani, just 33 years old, left behind two young kids and a pregnant wife.

Hani was among hundreds of Chaldeans held up and killed at their places of business over the years, with most of the crimes taking place in Detroit. While I slowly died inside prison, my family wept for the death of my brother, and there was nothing I could do to help.

In the depths of my bitterness, I still found the desire to survive. I knew that I not only had to use my rage and bodily strength, but I also needed my mind to be sharp. I read for leisure and to learn. I ordered as many books as I could and eventually received my GED diploma inside prison. I also started a college program while there. I wanted to get my bachelor's degree. I started corresponding with packets and books from a Michigan college. Professors from colleges would teach inside the prison's education building; some were good professors, and others were jerks.

Somewhere at the state level, it was decided to end the program inside Jackson. I was halfway through the program and never received my college degree. I really liked my computer class, but even when studying, I managed to get into fights. My computer class professor was a likable guy and so helpful. Despite his demeanor, as the old saying goes, when the cat's away, the mice will play—or, in this case, wreak havoc.

One afternoon, the professor stepped out to use the bathroom and warned the class not to open the door for anyone. Rod, a prisoner, standing 6'3" feet tall, with muscles like a bodybuilder, was with me in class that day. While waiting for the professor to return, we heard a knock on the door. Three prisoners were on the other side, asking the students inside to open the door. Rod, closest to the door, ignored the knocks.

They persisted and kept pounding their fists on the door and shouting for us guys inside to open it. One guy finally opened the door, and the three guys charged Rod. "What the F*** is wrong with you? Didn't you hear us telling you to open the door?" one guy shouted.

They kept cussing Rod out. I turned around because there was no way I wasn't going to respond.

"Hey, you continue, and it is going to get ugly for you," I said.

They looked at me and asked, "Who the F*** are you?"

"I am going to show you who the F*** I am."

I grabbed the fire hydrant off the wall and ran right for the first prisoner and slammed it on his head. The three prisoners ran out of the room, and I chased them down the hall with the fire hydrant. The chase was short-lived as the guards grabbed me and locked me up.

LOCKED IN RESENTMENT

The professor eventually returned to find the open door and half the class gone. After he inquired about what happened, he asked the guards to release me and allow me back in class.

Just another day in prison.

My routine to keep my mind mentally active and my body fit continued. I knew that, along with staying mentally sane, I had to stay in good physical shape. When we did get to go out of our cells, I worked out.

The prisoners had a gym inside and loose metal outside to lift weights. I worked out four days a week. I met some Chaldean guys, and we became friends. I also befriended an Italian prisoner named Ralph, who later died of cancer. One of the guys went back to prison after getting out for a while, and one is still serving a life sentence for killing an elderly lady. Inside, we were just friends who worked out together.

Along with feeling hopeless, prisoners claim innocence, too. Every prisoner thinks he is innocent. Yes, there are a few innocent people in prison, but I long ago stopped believing anyone who told me that they were innocent. Drug dealers seemed to get long sentences. They were in prison for years. Maybe they were not innocent, but, man, they were serving life sentences for dealing drugs. Days after the computer class incident, Rod talked to the guys who rushed into class. They told Rod that I was wrong. They began talking smack about me. All the Chaldeans inside were called "cousins" by everyone else. They repeatedly told Rod, "What your cousin did was wrong."

Rod began to panic, fearful of retaliation.

"Please, man, we need to squash this crap," he begged me.

FREEDOM BEHIND BARS

"Squash what? I will kill those guys. I am not squashing nothing," I said.

"Tom, I never met a crazy guy like you before. You got to calm down. You are going to kill somebody."

"I don't care. Better I kill them before they kill me."

That was life in Jackson. When I was not letting everyone know, I would kill them if they tried to instigate anything, I was reminded of what would happen if I didn't. Despite my outward appearance, I feared the torment that could occur. When I think of life doing time, certain images emerge. I vividly remember the darkness. Among the group of prisoners who preyed on the weak white boys was the guy I mentioned earlier, who we called Red. We would talk to each other between our cells when we were locked inside. Just remembering those disturbing conversations makes me retreat into darkness. Being inside prison walls is truly the definition of hell on earth.

My first prison transfer

While at Jackson, I was at a level 5—the highest level of security. I wanted to go to Ryan Correctional Facility in Detroit, which was closer to my family. They say to be careful what you ask for, and I learned that lesson. Before I was sent to Ryan, I was transferred to Huron Valley in Ypsilanti, where I was at a level 4. It was a much nicer prison, but I only lasted nine months there.

I knew that once I arrived inside the new prison, I had to make my mark as a madman. On my first day in Huron Valley, I called my family. While I was on the phone, about four to five guys approached me. They told me to get off the phone. It was their phone, they said. I turned around to see them better.

LOCKED IN RESENTMENT

"You are going to wait until I am done," I said.

"You better get off the phone or else," one of them yelled.

I noticed a prisoner I met in Jackson named Big John. He was a former biker who stood about 6'6" feet tall. I told Big John to watch my back until I got through on the phone. I finished my call with my sister Kathy, and I walked up to those guys.

"If you ever come up to me again, whether I am on the phone or anything else, I am going to beat your ass. I am going to show you who I am. You have no idea who you are messing with."

Big John walked up to me.

"Let it go, man," he said.

The guys walked away and never said a thing to me again.

Huron Valley was a small prison. There were two units with maybe 160 guys in each unit. There were also three units with guys who weren't mentally stable. They were locked up separately. I don't know why. No one inside prison ever seemed stable.

Officer Brooks was assigned to my floor. He hated inmates; he had it in for everyone. He would write up violations for no reason. He would fixate on a person until he wrote up enough violations to get him transferred to Jackson or to a worse prison. Brooks' wife worked in the control center; she was an attractive woman, and the prisoners often talked about her. All the inmates thought she was hot. Brooks was an older guy who looked like an ogre, with a wrinkled, scarred face.

Day after day, Brooks chose one inmate to harass. We always believed he planted items, such as weapons, on prisoners to get them in trouble. He would choose one inmate at a time and write that guy up every day. He claimed the prisoners threatened him.

Eventually, my turn came up. I had only been in Huron Valley for seven months. He went from cell to cell like going door to door. It was a joke, but no one did anything about it until Brooks decided to pick on me. It was just a game he played.

"Hey, Naemi," he said. "Your time has come."

"Brooks, you have no idea who you are about to mess with. I am going to become your worst nightmare. I am going to show you who I am."

"Yeah," he said. "We'll see about that."

The next day, I worked out in the morning, but before I went out, I asked two officers to inspect my cell, knowing all too well Brooks' tactics. The officers documented that my cell was clean and that everything was neat and organized.

The next day a sergeant told me I had a violation, and that Brooks wrote me up. According to the violation, Brooks gave me a direct order to clean my cell, and I didn't do it.

"No problem," I said to the sergeant. "I got this."

I retrieved the statement from the guards who inspected my cell and handed it over to the sergeant. I proved that Brooks was wrong, and I took the entire issue to a whole new level. I started to write up Brooks. I wrote him up for smoking too close to the cells; there was a rule that you had to be 25 feet away. I wrote him up for playing pool. Guards could not use inmate property or equipment. I wrote him up for putting our lives at risk because he was not in full

LOCKED IN RESENTMENT

security uniform most of the time. I would catch him sleeping and write him up. In one month, I wrote 150 violations against him.

I used my resentment toward Brooks and life in general to drive the guard crazy. However, not much happened. They didn't act because they all knew Brooks. I contemplated having my boys on the outside follow him and hit his car on the way home and beat him. I decided against it.

I continued to play the game. I beat him every time. He would time my showers every day, hoping I would go over. We had exactly 10 minutes, not a second more, to take a shower. He stood outside, timing me every day. I came out in nine minutes and looked at Brooks and said, "Oh, I had another minute to go."

"Get the F*** out of here, camel jockey!" he shouted at me.

"Oh yeah?" I said. "I guess I am going to have to write you up for racial slurs."

Brooks became enraged. He went ballistic and took all the pencils on his desk and started throwing them. He threw books across the room and inmate files of write-ups everywhere.

I stood at the door with complete calmness and watched as the guard created chaos in his own office. "Wow, what a mess you made! I guess someone needs to clean it up," I said as I walked away.

As I stood outside the door, porters walked into the office to clean it up and organize everything. I asked the officer in charge for five grievance papers, and I immediately began writing up Brooks. I complained that Brooks was harassing inmates for years, and they did nothing about it.

My family knew a senator in Lansing at the time, and I called him on a three-way call with a family member. I had them call about Brooks, the officer. I called my attorney and told him I wanted to act and sue Brooks and the state for allowing him to harass us.

While I waited to see what the senator and my attorney would do, I continued to play Brooks' game. Every time I saw him, I would make disparaging remarks about his wife, implying she was having affairs with other guards.

All the inmates were scared. They looked at me like I was crazy, but I didn't care. I was just beating him at his own game. A few days later, I got called into the office.

"Naemi, pack it up; you're leaving," said one of the officers.

Just like that, I was shipped off to the Ryan prison. They couldn't make one of Brooks' violations stick. Every time he wrote me up for a violation, I proved him wrong. I proved he was a liar. They eventually called Brooks into the office. He was transferred to night duty. The captain told him if he so much as looked at an inmate wrong, he would be fired.

Inside Ryan, I saw Drug Dealer Dan, whom I met on my walk into Jackson. He was surrounded by a group of massive men.

"Hey, it's Tom Naemi!" Drug Dealer Dan said. "You see this guy? He got more heart than anybody. I met this guy when we walked on the first day at Jackson Prison. He told me, 'Don't be afraid; anybody messes with you, I'll cut off his head and put it where the sun doesn't shine.' Look at him. I'd seen how small he was. I was like, 'This guy must get something that I don't know about.' Look how big he is."

LOCKED IN RESENTMENT

Dan had plans to get out of prison. He acquired a great deal of money over the years, and he always said he would go home long before I did.

"This lawyer is going to get me out, Naemi," he'd say. "It's going to cost me 25 grand, but he is going to get me out."

Sure enough, Dan was set free.

Be careful what you wish for?

At Ryan, I bunked with a cellmate who was chronically sick. His coughing kept me up the first night. He was also breathing heavily and throwing up. I get sick myself just seeing someone who is sick. Every day, I asked to get moved into a new cell. I couldn't deal with it. Every day, the counselor told me, "Tomorrow. Tomorrow, Mr. Naemi, we will move you."

Two weeks passed, and I had not slept. I was beyond aggravated; my resentment deepened, and the rage started to stir up. I wanted to kill somebody. "Tomorrow, my ass," I thought. The counselor was full of it.

My deep resentment for the counselor exasperated me so much that I carried my rage to her office, and I kicked the door in. It made a loud boom.

"You F'in' B*&#% I said. "You lied your way to the top, bending over to get this job, didn't you?"

She hit the panic button, and officers ran in. I was about to smash in her face. Suddenly, this really attractive sergeant, who used to talk to me, approached me to calm me down. I told her how much I wanted out of that cell, and she told me not to worry and that they would move me. I thought at the time she had the hots for me. Who knows?

FREEDOM BEHIND BARS

Despite my effort to silence my roaring rage, I was sent to the "hole"—solitary confinement. I was there for three months. They knew I was going to kill that witch. The hole was isolation, a cell with nothing in it but a bed and toilet. I slept well during those three months, and I did a lot of pushups as well.

One night, while in isolation, a sergeant approached me through a small window. Speaking with a heavy African accent, he began to talk to me.

"Hey, you," he said. "You are the one causing a lot of trouble, wanting to beat up people."

"Man, get the F*** out of here," I said. The officers were not supposed to come inside our cells.

"You think you're a tough guy?" he asked. "I will come in there and beat your ass."

"Oh yeah? What's stopping you, besides common sense and a good ass whooping?" I replied.

I was shocked. He put the key in the door and opened the door about two inches, and I leaped to my feet. I thought, "If this guy comes in here, I am going to beat him. It is me and him, one on one."

He locked the door. His voice shaking, he said, "Hey, Naemi. You are my kind of guy. I am going to take care of you. Whatever you want, let me know. I will get you the newspaper. Whatever you want."

He did. He took care of me the rest of the time I was there, and he even told the day sergeant to look out for me and take care of me, which he did. He said that they had messed with me, but I was a good guy.

LOCKED IN RESENTMENT

While in the hole, you only got 5-minute showers, and you were handcuffed walking into the shower. Whether or not you are soaped, clean or wet, you are done after five minutes. There was no drying off, and you were taken back to the cell naked.

They did get me the newspaper every day, though.

After three months, they moved me into a new unit and got me a new counselor. On my first day there, I was in line for breakfast. Some guy working in the food service department walked in front of me and said, "Come on, get that sugar out of your pocket."

"Hey, man, get the hell out of my face," I said. I had no idea what this guy's problem was, but he was accusing me of stealing sugar.

The guard tried to put his hand in my pocket, but I grabbed his hand and yelled, "You don't want me to beat you, do you? I am telling you, you aren't going to put your hand in my pocket. I got nothing in my pocket. Get the F*** away from me."

Seconds later, the morning sergeant walked in. I again grabbed the food service man's hand and shouted, "Don't you dare put your hand on me or in my pocket! You punk! There is nothing in my pocket."

The morning sergeant walked up to us. "Naemi!" he shouted. "Let him go."

"No, man," I said. "I am going to beat his ass. He thinks I stole something. This punk doesn't know who he is playing with."

Suddenly, the two started arguing. The sergeant called the food service guy a punk for harassing an inmate. The food service guy called the sergeant a punk for taking sides with an inmate. They went at it, and I walked away.

FREEDOM BEHIND BARS

All prisons are hell holes, but the Ryan prison was Satan's sacred place; it was full of drugs. We had 11 inmates escape in one night during the time I was there. The entire prison was a joke. People got killed; no one cared. When those prisoners escaped, they locked us in. They fed us when they felt like it. It got really ugly. When you are stuck in an 8-by-8 cell with another guy nearly 24 hours a day, imagine the insanity.

As I remember it, visitors waited hours to see inmates. Although it was the most horrendous of the prisons I had been in, I received good news during my time there. My sentence was reduced from 60 to 90 years to 15 to 40. My attorney proved in court that it was illegal to sentence me to 60 to 90 years for my crime. When the sentence was reduced, I had already served five years. When a prisoner serves one-third of his sentence, he qualifies for level 2 security.

So, I was reduced from level 5 to 4 and, finally, to 2. I could never go to level 1 because of my arson charge. After 10 years, I knew I could qualify for parole and eventually go home.

I was transferred to the Lapeer prison. I was living in resentment. I resented that my competitors tried to hurt my business. I resented getting caught trying to blow up their business. I resented being sent to prison. I resented being in prison. I could have lived in resentment for years if I hadn't found freedom in Christ.

Reflection on Resentment

I spent years resenting the situation I was in and blaming everyone for it. Yes, there are things done to all of us, but I failed to see my role in any of them. When we dwell on resentment, we literally lock ourselves in what happened to us - the past - instead of figuring out

LOCKED IN RESENTMENT

how to make the present better.

Making life better in an environment like a state prison is no easy task, but if I stayed in resentment, I would never find peace. I didn't realize at the time - while living in prison - that I needed to heal emotional wounds to be released from the prison of resentment.

Look at what you have read about my life so far. Resentment, like my other prisons, led me to this life behind bars. Resentment can trigger revenge and stir up anger and hatred in us, and we can find ourselves locked inside so many prisons within ourselves.

I didn't know at the time that emotional healing starts with taking up a relentless, persistent prayer to God. I wasn't even thinking about God, let alone praying to Him. Maybe that is your situation today. I not only had to forgive my enemies but also had to forgive myself. I had to pray for them and for myself. I had to lift my enemies up to the Lord for their own healing. I had to look deep within myself and honestly at my life to appreciate the negative. I am grateful I ended up locked up physically because it was there that I was released spiritually.

If I sat down with God face to face asking Him what to do with this resentment, I know He would tell me: Pray for the person who is making us angry. Pray for the situation that is causing me resentment. I know that we need to ask God to change us and to help us to get rid of our anger despite the rotten situation we are in. But we must do our part and start with ridding our mouths of anger, wrath, malice, slander, and obscene talk. We fight our resentment with the virtue of fortitude. We find courage, forbearance, strength, endurance, and the ability to confront fear, uncertainty, and intimidation. We forge ahead with faith in the Lord. With fortitude, we overcome our fear and are willing to take risks to follow Christ. A person with courage is willing to stand up for what is right in the sight of God, even when facing physical harm or death. I found my fortitude in prison, and slowly my resentment dissipated.

Do you find yourself in tense scenarios that could cause resentment?

- Being accused of something you did not do
- Having been put in a situation that is causing you stress
- Having been caught and punished for doing something wrong
- Having been lied to
- Having no support

Reflective Questions

1. What do you resent today?
2. What is causing the resentment?
3. How can you start praying to God to help heal that emotional pain that has caused the resentment?
4. How can the gift of fortitude help you release yourself from resentment?
5. How can your relationship with God strengthen your fortitude?

Bible verses to meditate on if you are locked in resentment:

If you forgive others their transgressions, your heavenly Father will forgive you. But if you do not forgive others, neither will your Father, forgive your transgressions (Matthew 6:14-15).

LOCKED IN RESENTMENT

But I say to you, whoever is angry with his brother will be liable to judgment, and whoever says to his brother, 'Raqa,' will be answerable to the Sanhedrin, and whoever says, 'You fool,' will be liable to fiery Gehenna. Therefore, if you bring your gift to the altar, and there recall that your brother has anything against you, leave your gift there at the altar, go first and be reconciled with your brother, and then come and offer your gift" (Matthew 5:22-24).

"He said to him, "You shall love the Lord, your God, with all your heart, with all your soul, and with all your mind. This is the greatest and the first commandment. The second is like it: You shall love your neighbor as yourself" (Matthew 22:37-39).

"That you should put away the old self of your former way of life, corrupted through deceitful desires, and be renewed in the spirit of your minds, and put on the new self, created in God's way in righteousness and holiness of truth" (Ephesians 4:22-24).

Chapter 7

LOCKED IN REVENGE

Finding Freedom in the Virtue of Forgiveness

"Tremble, and do not sin; Meditate in your heart upon your bed and be still" -Psalms 4:4.

±

It is almost a spontaneous reaction. I can't help it, and sometimes I don't know I am even doing it. I will erupt in song. I know people think I am crazy, but I can't help but walk around churches, the Eastern Catholic Re-Evangelization Center in Bloomfield Hills, Michigan, my own home — and just sing.

I love to sing Hallelujah, the Psalms, or a Christian song in my native tongue of Aramaic, but it is always praise to the Lord. This habit started in prison and never stopped, and I don't want to stop. Try it. It's so joyful and exhilarating to sing to the Lord.

Even in front of large crowds at events, I will sing—and not well. I am no Matt Maher or Chris Tomlin. But I am sure, just like them, my singing truly comes from a place of joy — something I never knew before I went to prison. You know by now that rage was my state of mind for most of my life. That is just who I was for the

FREEDOM BEHIND BARS

most part. I was angry deep inside my core, with a lion's roar ready to sound. That was my music for years.

In prison, the anger was slowly leaving my body. The lion's roar was beginning to fade, and music for the Lord was taking over. The desire to help people began to take over the urge to fight them. It wasn't prison itself that changed me. Most people who spend the years I did in prison are never able to survive in the outside world. Historically, prison changes a person for the worst, not the better. You can become more of a beast inside, but not me. No, it wasn't the prison walls that buried the lion; it was whom I met inside.

At this point, I was at the Thumb Correctional Facility in Lapeer, Michigan. While there, I attended church weekly. It was a Tuesday service. I figured, as a Catholic, why not go to church? It gave me something to do once a week that took me away from the daily pains of being incarcerated.

Without realizing it, my life was about to move in a direction I didn't know existed. I met all these Charismatics — these Holy Roller volunteers, as I used to call them. Charismatics are laypeople anointed in the Holy Spirit. They operate in the gifts of the Holy Spirit. I also met a prisoner named Roger, a Protestant who converted to Catholicism. He was serving natural life for murder.

During my time behind bars, I met many men who converted to Christianity in prison because they had time to study and pray.

When I met Roger, I was reading my books and thought, "Dear Lord, I could never be like this guy. This guy is amazing. How much knowledge does he have?" I figured God blessed him.

I met several volunteers, including deacons and a few women. Deacon Ed and his wife, Barbara, were so instrumental in my commitment to Christ. They were also Charismatics. Deacon Tom, too, led me onto a new path.

The volunteers held the weekly services as dedicated soldiers of Christ. These were the few moments in prison in which I found joy and peace. We read hymns and sang for about two hours every week. The first hour was mass, and the second hour was Bible study. We got to know everybody involved, including a few Chaldeans.

During one weekly service, I bumped into Deacon Ed in the halls; he engaged me in a conversation as I was leaving the service.

"How is your walk, Tom?" he asked.

"My walk is great. There is only one thing I got to do," I said as I walked away.

He caught it right away. He knew immediately to what I had been referring.

"Wait! Come back! Are you talking about revenge?"

"It may be revenge to you. I call it getting even."

"Wait a minute, Tom. Are you still harboring evil?"

"I am not harboring evil. I just have to even the score if it is the last thing I do."

"So, Tom, you don't know what it is like to be a Christian, do you?"

"What do you mean? Of course, I know what it is like to be a Christian."

In my mind, as I explained, a Christian is someone who professes Jesus as Lord, and that is it, but Deacon Ed knew I didn't grasp the full understanding of Christianity.

"Tom, let me tell you something. You have to forgive the people who hurt you."

"Well, that is easy for you," I said.

"No, it is not easy for me. That is what Jesus said."

"Well, it is easy for Jesus. I can't do it."

"You have to pray," urged Deacon Ed.

"How do I pray?"

"Ask Jesus to come between you and them."

I didn't know what that meant. It wasn't tangible to me. I couldn't see it or understand it, but I did exactly what the deacon asked me to do. I began to pray every day:

"Lord, help me overcome this anger. Come between them and me and take this anger away."

I did not know how to pray it any other way. In fact, I began to realize while I was saying those words that I had no idea how to pray at all. I prayed anyway, the best way I knew how.

I continued that very prayer for two years. It was far from an overnight change. I prayed even when I didn't see much change and even when I still felt hatred toward my enemies.

Meanwhile, life went on in prison and in the outside world. I often called home to check in. During one call, my family told me about a close relative of mine whose son, Lance, died while away at college. It was a Tuesday—worship service day. At the end of service, we sang, "I will raise you up on the last day."

I started to cry uncontrollably. My friend Big Ralph was next to me.

"Come on, buddy," he said. "Stop crying."

"I can't. This kid was like a son to me."

Big Ralph put his arms around me as the service ended. Mary, a volunteer, was leaving and began to talk to me.

"The Lord has a message for you," she said.

"What's the message?"

"Where there is death, there will be life. Where there is sadness, there will be joy, and the veil of ashes will fall off your face, and God is going to put a crown of glory on you."

"What does that mean?" I asked.

"I don't know," she said. "I only know I am to tell you this."

I thought she was smoking some bad bananas, or maybe I was going home. Those were the only two things I could think of because I really had no idea what she was talking about. On other days, Mary would bring her friend Michelle to pray with the prisoners.

One night, I had a dream I was preaching somewhere outside of prison. I was in church teaching about divine healing. The church was filled with my people—with Chaldeans. I could see many faces and families I knew. The Lord spoke to me in this dream: *"They don't believe I am God. They are going to die and go to hell."*

As I preached in a loud voice, the Lord spoke again to me: *"They don't believe I can heal them. They will die sick."*

My body was rising, and I was talking down toward the people. I woke up screaming in the night.

"Jesus is the healer!" I shouted from my cell. "Jesus is the healer!"

I woke up thinking I was going crazy. I had been locked up for too long. I was losing it.

The following Tuesday, I attended service and told Michelle about the dream. She told me to prepare because I was going to be a preacher.

"What are you talking about, Michelle? I don't know a thing about being a preacher. I don't know one thing about the Bible. How do you become a preacher?"

"It doesn't matter, Tom," she said. "What you don't know and what you do know doesn't matter. Jesus will do it through you. You just must surrender."

I looked at Michelle, and only one thought came to my mind.

"Whatever the Lord wants, let it be," I said.

Months passed, and it was now summertime. I started to have more dreams about Jesus.

I had a dream that I was walking on Drake Road in West Bloomfield, Michigan, but I didn't know what road it was in the dream. I saw a small hill, all nice and green. I saw someone's house. I knew it was a relative's house, although I had never seen it before. It wasn't even built at the time, I later discovered, but I saw it in my sleep.

In the dream, I walked into the kitchen and then into the hallway. I saw this beautiful picture of the Sacred Heart of Jesus. I admired it.

I even spoke to the picture, saying, "Lord, you really look good in this picture."

Jesus told me that my cousin was sick. *"He has pain on his left side. Tell him to drink a little red wine, and he will be healed."*

I saw the Lord, and his eyes and mouth were moving. Fear overcame me. I was really scared. The Lord said, *"Tom, don't be afraid. Listen to me. Tell your cousin not to worry. He worries too much. Tell him to drink a little red wine and tell him to stop worrying. Tom, don't forget. Tell your cousin to stop worrying. Drink a little red wine and stop worrying. He worries too much."*

He said it three times, and then I woke up and looked at the clock. It was 10 minutes to 4 in the morning. I had a dilemma: Should I tell my cousin about this dream?

I debated. If I told him and it turned out he was not sick, he would think I was delusional. If my cousin was sick and it was a message from the Lord, I would anger God for not telling my cousin.

I thought, "Maybe he is going to get healed. Maybe it is true. Maybe it is a revelation and not a dream."

I fell back asleep but woke up a short time later. I was too restless to fall back into a deep sleep. I woke up and walked over to the phone. They didn't open until 9 a.m. I had about 20 phone numbers with me in prison, and this cousin I dreamed about was one; we were also good friends.

I called.

"What's up, cousin?"

"You are early. What is going on?" he asked.

I never called anyone in the morning. The Lapeer prison operated efficiently and with a detailed structure. The prisoners did things on a schedule and in order. The warden walked around. It was a well-oiled machine. I asked my cousin if he had pain in his left side.

"Yeah, how did you know?" he replied.

"I got a message from the Lord Jesus. Do you believe in the Lord Jesus?"

"Yes, of course, I do."

"First, I got to tell you, I walked up to this house," I said. "It is this big white house with four pillars in the front. It has a beautiful brick and a marble floor."

"What are you talking about?" he asked. "I am building a house. I have the blueprints right now. I am building it on Drake Road."

"It is a beautiful house, cousin. I have already seen it."

"What? How?"

"I dreamed about Jesus. He told me to tell you to drink a little red wine. You are going to get healed. He told me you are worrying too much. Stop worrying."

Two months later, my cousin told me the pain was completely gone. Years later, when I was released from prison, my aunt, my mom's sister, died. People were paying their respects at my cousin's new home on Drake Road. I knew exactly where the home was located. I drove right up to the house. No one had to tell me how to get there or what it looked like.

A week after the phone call with my cousin, I had another dream. It was about a husband and wife. They were fighting. They were in a complete rage. Jesus told me to tell them, *"I hate divorce."*

LOCKED IN REVENGE

In the dream, I repeated to the couple what Jesus told me to say.

"Tell them they still love each other."

The couple was so angry they couldn't hear the Lord's voice.

So, I shouted louder: "The Lord says you both have this love in your heart, but you are both angry. You are overcome with your problems and your burdens. You are seeking a divorce, but divorce is not the answer. The Lord says, don't get a divorce. You love each other."

I suddenly woke up. It was 10 minutes to 5 in the morning. All the dreams I had about Jesus always happened at either 10 minutes before 4 a.m. or 10 minutes before 5 a.m. I knew that the Lord was sending me on a mission. The Lord told me about my cousin, and it was true. This had to be true, too.

I waited until 9 a.m. and called my brother Johnny to find the husband for me. I asked Johnny to tell the guy to answer his phone at 2 p.m.—that I would call. My brother told me to call a buddy of mine whom he knew had the number at 2, and he would set up the call.

At 2 in the afternoon that day, I phoned my buddy Zeke who had found the husband of this couple. On a three-way call, Zeke dialed the number. A three-way call was against prison rules, but I knew I had to make the call.

I had no time for small talk. I was in prison, after all, with a time limit on phone calls.

"You and your wife are contemplating divorce?" I asked.

"How do you know?" The man asked in a surprised voice.

"I am going to tell you, but you probably won't believe me. Last night, I had a dream about the Lord. He told me to tell you not to get a divorce and that you may have a lot of problems, but divorce is not the answer. The Lord told me you love your wife, and she loves you. You guys need to look into your hearts and find the truth."

The man was silent on the other line, but I continued.

"The Lord told me a story just in case you didn't believe me. He told me about something that happened the night before you got married. Something specific happened, right?"

The man didn't answer.

I repeated the story to him, all while Zeke was listening.

"Nobody knows about this incident except for you and your wife. Isn't that true?" I asked.

There was still silence on the phone.

"Hello?" I shouted. "You still there?"

"Yeah, I am here."

"Isn't it true?" I asked again.

"Yes, it is true."

"The Lord told me that when I tell you this story, you would believe me. What church do you go to? Who is the priest there?" I asked.

"I go to St. Thomas. The priest is Father Frank," he said.

"Go to him and get counseling."

I didn't know Father Frank at the time. I had no idea that he would one day become one of my biggest confidants and a bishop.

A week later, I had another dream.

I saw a man in a recliner with a bottle of Jim Beam in his hand. A young woman about 24 years old was standing behind his recliner. He looked like he was falling asleep. He was in his 60s. The Lord said to me, *"tell him it is his last chance. I have had enough with this guy."*

The Lord continued in a raised, powerful voice, *"I have given him so many opportunities. This is his last chance. I am fed up with this guy. Tell him this is his last chance. If he does not repent, he is going to go to hell forever. This is his last chance."*

The Lord's voice was stern. He was angry. I woke up in a sweat. I hadn't seen this man in years, even long before I went to prison. That morning I called Johnny again. This time I knew there was no reason to question whether or not to call this man. I truly believed these were messages from God.

"Johnny, you got to find this guy," I said. "Tell him I will call at 2 o'clock. We will put him on a three-way line."

At 2 that afternoon, I dialed my brother and again was on a three-way call.

"How are you doing?" I asked the man from my dream.

"I am doing good," he replied.

"You are not doing good. You don't have to lie to me."

"What? What are you talking about?"

"You are not doing good. You left your wife. I saw you last night."

I could hear the man's voice tremble. "What are you talking about?"

"The Lord let me see what you are doing. And He is not pleased with you. He told me to tell you that if you don't repent, you are going to die and go to hell soon."

"WHAT?" he screeched into the phone.

"Don't get mad. I am just the messenger. Last night, I saw you. You have a young girl living with you. She is about 24 years old. You drink Jim Beam every night. She is taking all your money. You are getting drunk, and you are falling asleep in that seat. The Lord is getting angry with you. If you don't repent, you will die and go to hell."

"What? Are you serious?" he asked loudly.

"Listen, brother. I haven't seen you in a long time. The last thing on my mind was you. The Lord wants you to listen to this Scripture. "If I say to the wicked, you shall surely die – and you do not warn them or speak out to dissuade the wicked from their evil conduct in order to save their lives – then they shall die for their sin, but I will hold you responsible for their blood (Ezekiel 3:18-19).

"Your blood is on your hands. The Lord said I had to tell you. I had to warn you. You better repent before it is too late. The Lord said, go back to your wife. Stop being a drunk and take care of your life. I am sorry I had to give you bad news, but it is not bad news if it saves your soul."

"Okay," he said.

"Think about it, man," I said before I hung up.

When I got out of prison and started preaching at various church events, that same man came to see me one night at a church

LOCKED IN REVENGE

in Oak Park. It was 2006. He walked up to me and kept talking about Jesus. "It is amazing how you changed your life," he said.

That same man was changed, too. I was so happy to hear that he went back to his wife.

A new journey had begun

Back in prison, I had another dream. I saw the Lord, and in that dream, I told Him that I love Psalm 1, Psalm 4, and Psalm 8.

I woke up and opened the Bible. I was not familiar with the Psalms.

I used to sleep with a pen and paper next to my bed in prison, just in case I got instruction from the Lord in my dreams. I didn't want to forget anything.

I wrote everything down.

There was no electricity when I woke up in the middle of the night. In prison, they cut off the power at 10 p.m. The only light I could find was outside my cell, but no prisoner was allowed outside the cell in the middle of the night. They never locked our cells at night, though, so I risked it. One early morning, an officer saw me walking outside his cell.

"What are you doing?" he asked.

"I am reading the Word."

"Why are you reading the Word now?"

"Because the Lord told me to read it."

"What?" asked the guard, with sarcastic doubt.

"I just got the word from the Lord that I should read Psalms 1, 4, and 8."

I walked outside and began reading the Psalms from my dream. The officer walked by as I read: "Blessed is the man who does not walk in the counsel of the wicked, nor stand in the way of sinners, nor sit in company with scoffers ... But not so are the wicked, not so! They are like chaff driven by the wind ... Ask of me, and I shall give thee the heathen for thine inheritance, and the uttermost parts of the earth for thy possession."

I had no idea what the words meant. I had no knowledge or understanding of Scripture. I could not comprehend any of it. I just kept thinking, "What does it mean? Why am I getting this message?"

Another week went by, and I told the Lord in a dream that I loved to read Psalm 10. In this dream, I also said, "Lord, I love to read Proverbs 28."

I woke up and realized I didn't even know there was a book of Proverbs in the Bible. I opened it and read Proverbs 28: "The wicked flee when no one is pursuing, But the righteous are bold as a lion."

I continued to read.

"I love those who love me; and those who diligently seek me will find me" (Proverb 8:17).

That week at church, the volunteers told us that they were going to host a seven-week seminar on "Life in the Spirit."

"Who wants to come?" they asked.

I was the first to raise a hand. I knew having all these dreams meant something, and I hoped the seminar would help me figure it

LOCKED IN REVENGE

out. I started to see a pattern - or, perhaps, destiny - come into play. I began to go to services because I hurt my back lifting weights. I used to deadlift up to 665. I injured my back during one lift routine, and I attended service to pray to heal my back. Week after week, I felt a strong desire to return. My heart was on fire, but I was barely walking. I was in pain, but I wasn't going back to be healed. I wanted to be spiritually uplifted. Something was happening to me from the inside out, but I didn't quite understand it at the time.

We prisoners had a variety of weights inside a fenced-in tent. We used to work out in the heat and cold. Only when it was higher than 100 or below 20 degrees would we not use the weight room. Otherwise, men lifted weights whenever they were able to go inside the tent.

The weights made prison even more dangerous than it already was because they could be used as weapons. Some guys' heads were cracked open. If inmates wanted to kill each other, they could find a way, and they did. Still, it was better for the prison that we did a workout. We released anger and stress when we lifted weights.

Meanwhile, my back continued to hinder me. One day during service, Mary, the volunteer, saw me and asked what was wrong.

"I hurt my back."

"Come here, let me pray on you," she said.

I looked at Mary with skepticism and said silently in my head, "Come on, lady. Who are you? You're not God. I don't want to embarrass you, but I am not letting you touch my back."

I believed the gift of healing is only for the apostles. No one has these gifts. With her hands on my back, Mary said, "In the name of Jesus, by the stripes of Jesus, you are healed."

I felt this immediate heat on my back. I felt a powerful surge in my body and wind that whirled around me with a loud buzzing sound. I felt electric shocks and big volts of electricity going through my back. "Oh my gosh," I thought. "This lady is for real." The prisoners then sat down for Bible study, and 10 minutes later, I jumped up and began to shout, "My back is healed!"

Like all prisons, the days were long at the Lapeer prison. I hung out with various jail mates who would become my friends inside. Rob was serving 24 to 40 years for killing his wife and his friend; the two were having an affair. I knew Rob from Jackson Prison, who was originally from Canada. Rob walked around in pain all the time. We were hanging out one day in the yard, and I saw that he was in pain, so I told him to come to church with me and get healing.

"Rob, there is this woman," I said. "You have to come see this lady."

"Shut up, Tom," he said. "You have lost your mind, man. You have been locked up for 10 years, and you have finally lost it."

"It is okay, Rob. You can say whatever you want, but have I ever lied to you?"

"No, man."

"Then come to service one time. See this lady."

"Oh, shut up, Tom."

Rob stood more than 6 feet tall.

"Has my little friend lost his brain?" he asked.

"Rob, just come one time."

He finally came to service, and Mary prayed for him. The next day, he was in the weight room, lifting weights and jogging. From that moment, I truly believed. I knew there was such a thing as a healing gift, and God wanted people to have it. God wanted me to have it, even though I didn't know it at the time.

I woke up in the middle of the night again, and I was preaching divine healing. It was a dream. In my dream, I woke up to read, and I was preaching in a room filled with Chaldean people I didn't know. I know it sounds crazy. I had a dream that I was dreaming.

The Lord spoke to me in the dream.

"You see all these people, Tom? They do not believe that I am God, and they are going to die with sin."

I began preaching with such conviction. My voice raised.

"Jesus is God. Jesus is the way. If you want to get to God, you must go through His Son. Jesus is the Lord. He is God. He is the second person of the trinity."

As I stood there preaching, Jesus was talking to me.

"They do not believe that I am God. They do not believe that I can heal them."

I started preaching even louder. "Don't you know that Jesus can heal you? Don't you know that He is God? He is our savior? It takes the faith of a mustard seed."

In the midst of my screaming, my lungs shut down. I felt like

FREEDOM BEHIND BARS

I couldn't breathe, and then I woke up. I thought to myself, "Oh Lord, I am going crazy. I have lost my mind. I was shouting in my sleep.

I looked up at the bunk above me to see my cellmate. I worried I had woken him. If he woke, he would have seen me totally distraught and almost in tears. Something was happening inside of me now. Something profound and deep. I didn't recognize the rage of the lion that once consumed my soul. It began to dissipate. There was this sense of peace and joy in my heart. These were the same prison walls I had lived behind for years. The same jail cells. The same bars. The same guards. The same inmates. Every jail I was locked up in was the same, but the Tom Naemi that walked inside those cell doors nearly 10 years ago was fading.

The anger was nearly gone. I no longer thought about killing my competitors or even thought of having a real enemy. I used to play this plot in my head repeatedly — that one day, I would walk in with boys from the neighborhood, and they would stage a fake holdup, steal from my competitors, and eventually kill them.

Transforming inside prison walls

That is what I thought about every day for nine years. During this 10th year in prison, a transformation took place. This was when I started to find my freedom. This was the year I was breaking away from the shackles inside my soul, even though my body remained behind bars.

One night, before they cut the power at 10 p.m., I was flipping through the channels, staring at my 10-inch black-and-white TV. I saw this preacher, R.W. Schambach, who asked, "Do you know Jesus, or are you just a churchgoer? Do you know Jesus? Even the devil can go to church, but do you really know Jesus?"

LOCKED IN REVENGE

With those words, the power turned off.

I sat on my bottom bunk thinking of how I attended church for 34 years, yet I never knew Jesus. I used to think that if I did my duty every week, went to church, and threw $50 to $100 in the basket as a reward to the Lord, I could live like the devil Monday through Saturday.

When I tell this part of my testimony, people always laugh.

"You laugh—I know," I say to them, "but it is true, and maybe you do the same."

About five minutes later, after I thought about my past life, I could feel myself sitting taller on my bunk as I straightened my back and spoke out loud. "Lord, I don't know how I am going to do this, but today I am giving you, my life. You already know that I messed up my life pretty good. I had everything, and now I have nothing, but from now on, I give you, my life. Use me any way you want. I know you will do a better job than what I have done."

The next morning when I woke up, I felt a deep sense of freedom as if I was walking along a beach, looking at the waves, with no worries in life. I felt pure happiness, and not one drop of anger ran through my body. I no longer felt frustrated. Instead, peace settled deep inside my being.

Days later, the volunteers nominated me, along with my prison mate Tim, to oversee the Catholic Group. I didn't want to be nominated. I tried to get out of it and tell them to have Tim do it, but they insisted, "No, it was going to be Tom and Tim."

I pulled Tim aside.

"Tim, I don't know much about Scripture. This is what I will do. You take care of the Scripture readings, and I will clean up after the inmates. I will do the setup. I will have the altar and chairs ready."

That is exactly what we did.

We had service for one hour and then Bible study after. Every week, nearly 45 men sat in a circle to talk about Scripture. While I sat one day, I looked up at the ceiling and believed I could see Heaven open like drapes opening across a window. I saw Jesus sitting on the throne like a mighty king.

I could see the features were of Jesus, but I couldn't see his face completely because He was beaming with light in His glory. He was shining brighter than the sun. I looked intensely at the image of Christ and spoke silently to Him: "Lord, I am not telling anyone what I am seeing because they are going to take me out of here into a straitjacket and directly to a mental institution."

I then saw a laser light come down from Heaven and beam to my own heart. At that moment, I knew God. I truly understood God. He was infinite love. In a split second, He showed me hundreds of horses running in an open field. The fields were green, but the horses were different colors. He showed me how much He enjoyed every horse in its own color. They were spotted, gray, red, white, and brown; I knew God loved each one of us, even in our differences. I was overwhelmed with love.

I began to weep, but I didn't want the other inmates to see me in tears. I wanted to run out of the room, but the volunteers asked if I had anything to say.

"I have nothing to say today," I replied.

I left that Bible study with tears still streaming down my face.

LOCKED IN REVENGE

I knew I was preaching in my dreams. I knew I needed to learn. These dreams could be for nothing, and now I was certain they were not.

All the inmates who signed up for the seminar studied every day. Three of us would sing, and two played the guitar. I felt immense joy every time the music played. It was the first time in my life that I was truly happy. I so desperately wanted to share what I now had with others. I started approaching the young prisoners. I promised if they came to church, I would protect them. I still had this reputation as a crazed man who would kill anyone who messed with me, so I knew I could offer protection. Getting them to go to church was my bargaining tool.

"I have your back, guys," I would say in my mad man's voice. "I won't let anyone touch you. I will crack anyone's head who messes with you."

Although it sounded crazy while I uttered those words to those young prisoners at risk of being raped by other prisoners, the joy was overflowing. I was so happy. I believed that if I could get these men to go to service, they would turn their lives over to Christ.

After 10 years in prison, it was common for inmates to freak out. I was certain many people thought that what was happening to me was insanity. I could just imagine others saying, "Tom Naemi is going more nuts than he already was before he entered the prison gates."

In reality, I was waking up every day happy. I was trying to convert people. I wanted to talk about Jesus. That alone made me seem looney. Every opportunity I had, I used it to talk about Scripture and the Lord.

Inmates used to wash clothes for the local hospital. They used industrial-sized washers that stood about 10 feet tall. Every morning

FREEDOM BEHIND BARS

I had my same breakfast — peanut butter and honey with instant coffee. While I was eating, a Jewish prisoner who worked in the laundry walked up to me and asked if I would like to buy a rosary.

"Yeah, where did you get it?" I asked.

"I found it in the wash."

"What do you want for it?"

"Give me $4."

"Gladly," I said.

I knew it was another sign. I ran up to my cell and took out $4 in stamps I had stashed. It was currency inside prison. Two and a half years after I started preaching, I had a dream, and Jesus gave me a gift. I saw Jesus in an open field, and He was glowing and wearing a white outfit. I knelt before the Lord.

"I have a gift for you, Tom," Jesus said as He gave me a rosary.

"Lord, this is my rosary."

"But I am giving it to you, Tom."

"But Lord, it is already my rosary."

"But I am giving it to you, Tom."

"But it is already mine."

"And I am giving it to you."

"Okay, Lord."

I took it from Him. I believed that the Lord wanted to let me

LOCKED IN REVENGE

know He was going to bless me with a gift. I started to pray the Rosary with my cellmate. We prayed the Rosary every day and read the Psalms. But I still couldn't understand the Bible. It was so difficult for me to comprehend. One day I really struggled with it. The next day I went to church.

The volunteers announced they would be hosting the "Life in the Spirit" seminar for seven weeks for one hour following our regular mass on Tuesday. I was the first one to raise my hand. During this time, I went deeper into the Spirit, joy, peace, and happiness. My dreams became more intense. In a dream, I went to heaven with Archangel Michael. I felt like I left my body. I was in a tunnel, and I saw the light. It was the beaming light of God. Michael tied my tongue. He said I talked too much and that I needed to listen. I was standing in front of the Lord, singing in Aramaic, my native tongue. I was dancing in front of the Lord. I was screaming, "I am here. I am finally here." I woke up singing. I was in a great ecstasy of joy the entire time. I can't describe it in words.

After the seven-week seminar, a young Polish priest was celebrating actual mass, which was rare. It was the first time I met Father John. He said, "I don't have time to hear everyone's confession, but if you tell me your biggest sin, I will give you absolution."

It was my turn.

"I have been arrogant my whole life, and I want the Lord to humble me."

He placed his hands on me and prayed on me.

Then a group of 13 men walked in and broke up into smaller groups and started to pray on people. I went to the first group. They

FREEDOM BEHIND BARS

laid their hands on me. I felt the left side of my body go numb. I didn't break out in tongues or fall out in the Holy Spirit, which is not uncommon, but an enormous sense of peace came over me. Falling out or resting in the Spirit is when the Holy Spirit overcomes you, and you actually pass out.

When I ran away to Iraq, an older priest used to sing the Psalms in Arabic. Inside the prison, as they prayed on me, I knelt and started to sing just as the priest had sung.

I looked up and noticed that one group had no one to pray on, so I figured it couldn't hurt to get prayed on again. The volunteers, Mary and Michelle, were in this group.

"Didn't you get prayed on already?" Michelle asked.

"Yes, but I am thirsty for the living water," I said, not even knowing what these words meant. They smiled because they knew what it meant, but they were aware that I didn't know. They prayed on me once more.

After the 13 prayer volunteers left, we prisoners sat around asking each other how we all felt. Everyone said nothing changed, but my entire life was changing. The man I used to be was about dead, and the new Tom was being born.

The next day, I prepared my peanut butter and honey and poured hot water for coffee. Each one of the two of us inside the cell had a desk, and we shared one TV. I was watching BBC, and they were reporting on Iraq. The next word I heard was God, and a wind gust whipped through my cell. I felt a massive breeze like a windstorm. I knew it was the Holy Spirit. My body temperature rose. I felt as though I was on fire, like the time I tried to blow up my competitor's store.

I stood up and screamed, "Jesus is in the house! Get up! Jesus is here!"

I felt pain. I felt the nail marks on my hands. I felt a hole in my heart.

My cellmate, also a Chaldean, turned around and started speaking to me in our native language.

"What is wrong with you?" he asked. "Daywana (are you going crazy on me)?"

"Yeah, man, I am crazy. I told you that you should have come to the Life in the Spirit service. Feel my body. I am on fire."

"Oh my gosh! Your hands are on fire!" he said.

"I know, man; Jesus is here. I told you to come with me. Get up. I am going to pray on you."

This cellmate always had ankle problems.

At that moment, I heard a voice tell me repeatedly to "open the book."

I started to pray on my cellmate's ankle, saying, "By the stripes of Jesus, you are healed."

I turned as I was praying. The entire time the Bible was on my desk next to me. I bought this new American Bible and thought, "Oh my gosh, this Bible is talking to me."

I opened it, and it was John.

"Jesus answered, "Amen, amen, I say to you, no one can enter the Kingdom of God without being born of water and Spirit" (John 3:5).

FREEDOM BEHIND BARS

In a second's time, the Scripture came to life. I felt a true anointing. "This was a love story between God and me," I said to myself. "How could Nicodemus understand it? He was flesh like me. Now all those dreams make sense."

Nicodemus is from John Chapter 3; the high priest comes at night to ask Jesus what he must do to inherit the Kingdom of Heaven. Jesus tells him that he must be born again of water and the Holy Spirit. Jesus goes into a deep explanation of the Spirit. Nicodemus doesn't get it.

I had flashbacks of my dreams. I began to scream out in my cell and recite Bible verses in excitement.

I shouted words from Matthew 6:33: "Seek first His kingdom and His righteousness," and Psalm 1: "When you bless the Lord, He will bless you."

Now it all made sense. I acknowledged to the Lord that I understood it. That night I read the Bible for at least six hours. The next day, I read the Gospel of John.

Jesus and Nicodemus were having a conversation. Now I truly understood that Jesus was talking about the trinity. Most people don't' get it when they read it.

"Ruha" in Aramaic means "wind" and "holy spirit." Nicodemus thinks Jesus is talking about the wind, but he is really talking about the Holy Spirit from Heaven. Jesus tells him that he must surrender if he wants to know Him. You cannot comprehend Him unless you become spiritual. There is a realm — body, soul, and spirit.

The next day I read the Bible for more than five hours. In an instant, I saw a video of Genesis. I heard God's voice: *"See how much I love man. I am a God of love. I don't want man to come to me like a robot or like a dog."* God spoke to me in my ghetto slang just so I could understand.

"I want him to come to me out of free will. If he rejects me, I respect him and leave him."

I began to scream out in my cell again: "Now I know you, God. I know you are a God of love. How can people know you and not love you?"

This occurrence was happening to me every day. I would read the Bible, and every day more was revealed to me. I began to truly understand God and Scripture. I began to know Christ.

I was on fire for Jesus. I was anointed two weeks before Christmas. This idea of being anointed is foreign to many, including many Christians. I share my testimony knowing this anointing to be true. I was anointed with knowledge of the Scripture and a healing ministry.

After I started reading the Bible, I was not running to the weight pit anymore. No one in prison recognized me. My old friends began to question me.

"Who are you, man?" they would ask.

"I am Tom; what are you talking about?"

"No, man, you ain't Tom. Who are you? You are reading the Bible all day. You are a Bible thumper. We don't know you."

"You wouldn't understand. There is something greater," I said.

"Come on, Tom. Who has time for this nonsense?"

"It is nonsense to you because you do not understand. It is beyond the world's comprehension what has happened to me."

"You used to make fun of these guys. You used to cuss them out, and now you have become one of them?"

"Yeah, I have become one of them."

One of my old friends I used to pump iron with begged me to hang out in the weight room. "No, Ricky, I am done with that," I said. "I am now praying. People are being healed."

This was all happening in the year of 1999 to 2000. My friends continued to express their frustration as I further distanced myself and prayed in solitude.

One afternoon, I decided to join them inside a small room in prison. There were about 25 guys in the room. They had a small TV. They were watching the Pistons play basketball. Another inmate named Zeke, a few cells down from me, complained about his wrist.

"I cannot even hoop anymore," he said.

I heard God's voice telling me to pray for Zeke. I began a conversation with God in my mind.

"Now Lord, you know if I go pray for him, they are going to think I am crazy."

"Go pray for him," God replied in a stern voice.

"Okay, Lord, don't get mad," I thought.

"Zeke," I called out. "Do you believe Jesus can heal you?"

The entire room of 25 men laughed in unison.

"Oh my gosh, that boy has lost it," one guy shouted.

"He be crazy," said another.

I grabbed Zeke's wrist and proclaimed, "By the stripes of Jesus, your wrist is healed."

The next day Zeke ran into my cell screaming, "Tom, I hooped today! My wrist is healed!"

After that, I started to change my daily routine. I woke at 5 a.m. so I could have time with Jesus before everyone else in prison got up. I prayed. I read Scripture, and my life began to change drastically.

I did eventually go back to the weight pit. I had to maintain a certain strength to protect myself and the guys I promised to protect. I didn't want to spend too much time with other prisoners. I wanted to get back to the Bible. I stopped using profanity. I didn't want that garbage to come out of my mouth anymore. The conviction of the Holy Spirit was now in my heart. I felt a knife pierce my heart any time a bad word passed my lips.

One afternoon, I saw Zeke in the bathroom. Another prisoner, Kip, was there. He had a sling on his arm and had torn up his shoulder. Kip was screaming.

"Tom," Zeke called.

"Yes, brother Zeke?"

"If you pray on him, he will be healed."

"Thou shall not cast what is holy to dogs," I said. "That dog is not worth the gift of God."

Kip was a devil worshiper.

"No, brother Tom," said Zeke. "If you pray for him, he shall be healed."

Despite my doubts, I complied.

FREEDOM BEHIND BARS

"Okay, if you say so."

I then kicked the door in. Kip was in the cell next to mine.

"Come out, Kip."

"Shut up and come out," I yelled back.

"No, man, I can't move," he yelled.

Zeke put his hand on Kip's left side, and I placed my hand on his other side, and we began to pray. Zeke started vomiting.

"Lord, I give you the glory and in the name of Jesus ..." I continued.

Before I finished, Kip started screaming, "Oh my God! My arm is healed! I have no pain!"

Several men from the block ran over. Kip removed his sling and headed back to his cell to smoke.

"I can't believe it. I went to the hospital. They give me pain killers, and I come here, and I get healed," he said.

Everyone started talking and could not believe it. Some started to praise God. Then Kip returned to where I had been.

"You know, Tom, I was thinking," he said. "Before you prayed for me, I took about 20 painkillers. You don't think the Motrin kicked in?"

I became angry and had this rage that made me think of ripping Kip's head off his body. It was righteous anger because I was angry for the Lord.

"You are a punk. You are a dog. You don't deserve God's healing. You unbeliever. Don't come back to me when your pain comes back," I said.

LOCKED IN REVENGE

Zeke, all puked out, approached me.

"Tom, when we prayed on him, I felt sick," he said. "It tasted like rotten egg."

"That's because we prayed the demon out of him," I said.

Reflecting on the prison cell of revenge

I started out locked in revenge, and through Christ, I was released from that prison. I no longer had hatred toward those I perceived as my enemies. In fact, I began to pray for them and for healing between us.

Hebrews 12:15 says, "See to it that no one be deprived of the grace of God, that no bitter root spring up and cause trouble, through which many may become defiled."

That bitter root stays in our hearts and minds. It did for me. Every day for more than a decade, all I could think about was how I was going to get even with my enemies. Revenge boiled in my belly. I thought about it every day, even in my sleep. I used to wake up in a cold sweat imagining fighting with them. I carried the demons of hate for a long time.

I could not be set free until I was told by Deacon Ed to forgive them and to pray. I prayed for almost two years that Jesus would take that feeling from me, and the Lord did. I was released from the pain that I had carried for years.

Restoration and rationality came into the picture, and I became a positive person instead of an angry one—one who can accomplish things instead of one who can't do a thing. My prayer was, "Lord Jesus, I ask you to come between these people and me. Take all hatred away from me and bless them." I had to forgive my ene-

FREEDOM BEHIND BARS

mies to find freedom. It is the virtue of forgiveness that releases us from the vice of revenge.

I turned the tide on the enemy, and I was set free. I never looked back. I was so excited about the future from that point on because great things were about to happen. Even if you don't act on revenge, wishing harm on someone is vengeful. The intent in our heart could darken it, hurt our soul and disconnect us from God. We cannot desire to harm others even when they harm us. God calls us to love our enemies and pray for them.

Revenge, whether carried out or not, serves no purpose at all. Don't seek revenge. "Vengeance is mine," says the Lord. Let go and let God take over. It is the only way to find freedom. It is through the virtue of forgiveness that we are released from revenge. I had to forgive my enemies and myself. Scripture teaches us must forgive others and ask for forgiveness. "Be kind to one another, tenderhearted, forgiving one another, as God in Christ forgave you." The Good News: Don't forget that we receive forgiveness and, in turn, should be kind and forgiving to those around us. "The Lord has forgiven you, so you also must forgive."

Do you find yourself in these scenarios where you could seek revenge on someone?

- Someone stole from you or lied about you
- Someone hurt your business or livelihood in some way
- Someone harmed a family member or loved one
- Someone prevented something good from happening for you
- Someone made a decision that was made with bad intent

Reflective Questions

1. How seeking revenge be harmful to me and others?

LOCKED IN REVENGE

2. Who do I want revenge on?
3. Instead of seeking revenge, what could I do from a Christian perspective to release myself?
4. Who must I forgive?
5. How can I start to forgive those who hurt me?

If you are locked in revenge, here are some Scripture verses to reflect on:

God is the only Judge and He will exact Judgment (Hebrews 10:30-31).

Never take your own revenge, beloved, but leave room for the wrath of God, for it is written, "VENGEANCE IS MINE, I WILL REPAY" says the Lord (Romans 12:19).

Wait for the LORD for He will help you. (Proverbs 20:22).

Where is their God? Before our eyes, make known among the nations that you avenge the outpoured blood of your servants (Psalms 79:10).

But I say to you, love your enemies, and pray for those who persecute you, that you may be children of your heavenly Father (Matthew 5:44-45).

Chapter 8

LOCKED IN ADDICTION
Finding Freedom in the Virtue of Temperance

"And you shall serve the Lord your God, and he shall bless your bread, and your water; and I will take sickness away from the middle of you"-Exodus 23:25.

±

When people try to overcome an addiction, they often replace it with another.

We all know people who stop smoking, only to gain weight. I guess you could say I was addicted to fights. Being locked in anger and hate led me to constantly want to brawl.

It was through Christ that I was freed.

In prison, I realized I had to help others with their own addictions, and one man needed to be released before I could ever go home. The inmates were becoming angry with me. I was sharing my revelations from God – my dreams and this upset a lot of people. At this point, the volunteers kept asking me what God was telling me.

The Catholic group became upset with me, claiming that I was trying to take over. They walked over to me one service day and I could tell they were angry.

"What's going on?" I asked.

"You are trying to take over with all your talk about revelation and God talking to you," they said.

"Take over what? What do you guys have that I am trying to take over?"

"Our work."

"I am not trying to take over nothing. You guys are clowns. You don't want to hear the word of God; You can have your service. I will not reveal anything to you anymore."

And I walked away. The next week I decided to go back to Catholic service. The volunteers were excited, and they wanted me to talk.

"Come on, Brother Tom — what do you have to share with us this week?"

"Nothing."

"Why? We want to hear."

"Thou shall not cast what is worthy to dogs. There are a lot of dogs here and I cannot share it with them."

"Come on, Brother Tom."

"No, I am not going to talk."

Service ended and the group started singing "Amazing Grace."

LOCKED IN ADDICTION

As soon as they started to sing, my body heated up and I felt I was going to start to ooze like a volcano. I heard a *"fsh-fsh-fsh"* sound. "I feel the Holy Spirit is here," I said to my cellmate. "I feel an anointing. My head is about to pop."

He felt my back. "Yeah, man, you are burning up," he said.

The group then started to sing "Here I Am, Lord." I began singing the words, "I will go Lord, if you lead me," and as I raised my hand, I felt the palm of God on my heart.

"Okay, God, I am going wherever you lead me," I whispered as the group sang.

My face was flushed. I began to glow. When I left service, all of the other men were looking at me and then started to back away.

"Tom, you are beaming, man," one of them said.

"Your lights are on. You are shining." another observed.

They looked so scared.

"What is wrong with you guys?" I asked.

I walked to the bathroom to look in the mirror. My face was bright red, as if I had just run 10 miles in the heat. I realized why the men reacted the way they did. I couldn't believe what I saw myself. I knelt and began to talk to God.

"Thank you, Lord. I know that I will be leaving prison soon."

Continuing the ministry

That night I had a dream. I was praying with men who had no faces. They were black silhouettes. They were all standing and praying. When I woke up, I knew that I was being sent to a new prison. I sat

FREEDOM BEHIND BARS

down to have my regular breakfast. I was pouring the hot water when I heard an officer shout my name.

"Naemi!"

"Yes, sir?" I responded as I turned around.

"Today is your last day here."

"I know, sir."

"How do you know?"

"The Lord already told me that today is my last day here."

He rolled his eyes. "Whoever told you ... well, pack it up. In a couple of hours, you will be leaving."

I walked back to my cell and packed up. I was thinking about how in prison everyone is just a commodity ; no one has a say in his own life. Each person is just a number — barely a human being.

And, just like that, I moved. I was sent to the Pine River Correctional Facility in St. Louis, Michigan. It was February 2000.

My ministry while in prison was my entire focus. I had a clear purpose, and the first thing I did when I entered Pine River was to inquire about Catholic service. I quickly discovered that they did not offer a Catholic mass. I didn't want to waste any time, so I took it up with the prison chaplain.

"We have to have Catholic service," I demanded of the chaplain.

"Well, we don't. We have four Protestant services. If you can sign up 11 men, you can start your own service," he said.

I was on mission. I needed to find at least 11 Catholic men

LOCKED IN ADDICTION

in this prison so I could start a new service. I decided to write a note to the chaplain, stating that I was determined to have a Catholic service.

The chaplain responded in writing: "We do not have Catholic service."

I already knew that, but what the chaplain didn't seem to understand was that I wanted to start one as soon as possible and would, in fact, have those 11 men.

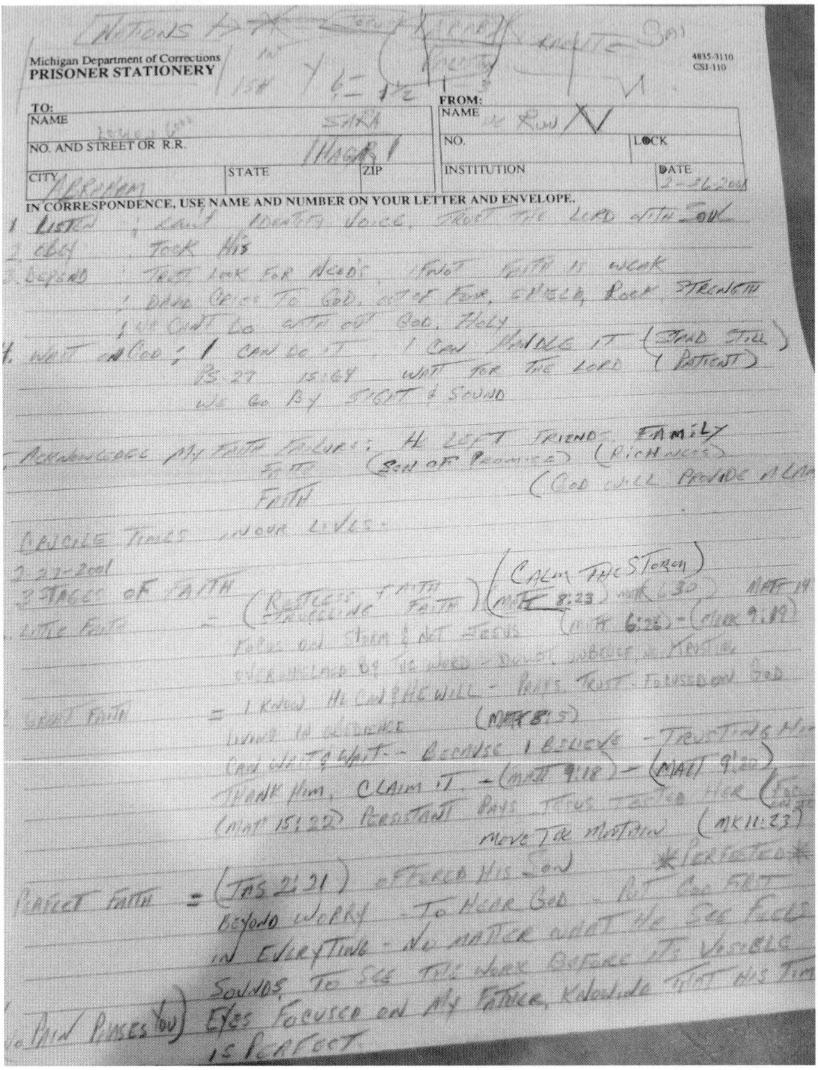

Michigan Department of Corrections
PRISONER STATIONERY

4835-3110
CSJ-110

TO:
NAME SARA
NO. AND STREET OR R.R. HAGAR
CITY ABRAHAM
STATE
ZIP

FROM:
NAME
NO.
LOCK
INSTITUTION
DATE 2-26-2001

IN CORRESPONDENCE, USE NAME AND NUMBER ON YOUR LETTER AND ENVELOPE.

1 LISTEN ; IDENTIFY VOICE, TRUST THE LORD WITH SOUL
2 OBEY TOOK HIS
3. DEPEND ; TRUST LOOK FOR NEEDS, FAITH IS WEAK
; CRIES TO GOD, FEAR, SHIELD, ROCK, STRENGTH
; WE CAN'T DO WITH OUT GOD, HOLY
4. WAIT ON GOD ; I CAN DO IT, I CAN HANDLE IT (STAND STILL) (PATIENT)
PS 27 15:64 WAIT FOR THE LORD
WE GO BY SIGHT & SOUND

ACKNOWLEDGE MY FAITH FAILURE; HE LEFT FRIENDS FAMILY
FAITH (SON OF PROMISE) (RICHNESS)
(GOD WILL PROVIDE A LAM
FAITH

CRUCIAL TIMES IN OUR LIVES

2-27-2001
3 STAGES OF FAITH
LITTLE FAITH = (RESTLESS FAITH / STRUGGLING FAITH) (CALM THE STORM) (MATT 8:23) (6:30) MATT 14
(MATT 6:26) - (MARK 9:18)
FOCUS ON STORM & NOT JESUS
OVERWHELMED BY THE WORD - DOUBT, UNBELIEF
GREAT FAITH = I KNOW HE CAN & HE WILL - PRAYS, TRUST, FOCUSED ON GOD
LIVING IN OBEDIENCE (MARK 8:5)
CAN WAIT & WAIT - BECAUSE I BELIEVE - TRUSTING HIM
THANK HIM, CLAIM IT - (MATT 9:18) - (MATT 9:20)
(MATT 15:22) PERSISTANT PRAYS JESUS TESTED HER
MOVE THE MOUNTAIN (MK 11:23)
PERFECT FAITH = (JAS 2:21) OFFERED HIS SON *PERFECTED*
BEYOND WORRY - TO HEAR GOD - PUT GOD FIRST
IN EVERYTHING - NO MATTER WHAT HE SEE FEELS
SOUNDS, TO SEE THE WORK BEFORE ITS VISIBLE
PAIN PASSES YOU) EYES FOCUSED ON MY FATHER, KNOWING THAT HIS TIME
IS PERFECT

LOCKED IN ADDICTION

Notes Tom wrote while in prison.

FREEDOM BEHIND BARS

LOCKED IN ADDICTION

INTRAMURAL CORRESPONDENCE
4835-3105
CSJ-105 12/96

Name: Grace   No.: _____   Date: _____
Assignment: _____   Lock: _____

1. Is God's Kindness & Graciousness without Merit or Earnings - Love

2. Gift without Work
Cannot be paid back, can't be purchased
We got more to get Grace - Jesus took care of that by Faith.

STEPS THAT FALL AWAY - BACKSLID
1. Desire (sin) wants to live his
2. Descion (sin) made up his mind
3. Departure (sin) left on his own
4. Description (sin) Satan paint a better picture
5. Defeat (sin) lost all with loose living
6. Despair (sin) lost his respect, dignity
7. Desperation (sin) in need of all things

Faith
EPH 2:8 By Grace without work or merit, Gift
TITUS 2:7 in all things
TITUS 2:14 to redeem us & purify us
TITUS 3:1 Be ready to every deed
TITUS 3:8 to devote themselves to do good

FREEDOM BEHIND BARS

INTRAMURAL CORRESPONDENCE
4835-3105
CSJ-105 12/96

Name: Catholicism and Fundamentalism   No.: _____   Date: 9-18-2000
Assignment: By Karl Keating   Lock: _____

Missing Books 1

Tobit, Judith, Wisdom, Ecclesiasticus, Baruch
and Maccabees 1 & 2
Also part of (Esther 10:4 to 16:29)
         Daniel 3:24-90 and Chapter 13 & 14

Oral Tradition
1 Cor 15:3, 11 (2 Tim 2:2) Thes 2:15 (Jn 14:16)
Eph 3:5 (Eph 2:20) Lk 10:16 (Is 59:21) Acts 2:42
Mat 28:19 (Malachi 2:7)

Tradition   (Mt 15:3 Human)
            (Col 2:8 Church)
Purgatory Lk 12:59 (1 Pet 3:19)

I would need to order
1   Catholic Encyclopedia (1914 edition best)
     or 1967 edition
and Catholic Commentary on Holy Scripture
     Published in Britain 1953. Douay-Rheims

Your Servant

LOCKED IN ADDICTION

> **INTRAMURAL CORRESPONDENCE**
> 4835-3105
> CSJ-105 12/96
>
> Name: NAEMI   No.: 210051   Date: 2-29-2000
> Assignment: _____   Lock: F-79
>
> I would like to see you about Catholic services, please help me set up this place, and I would like to assist you in any way possible.

FREEDOM BEHIND BARS

> **INTRAMURAL CORRESPONDENCE**
> 4835-3105
> CSJ-105 12/96
>
> Name: **PRIDE**   No.:   Date: 5-29
> Assignment: **HUMBLE ME LORD**   Lock:
>
> 1. POSSESIONS - Give away, Give to God, Bless
> 2. POSITION - Aknowledge God gave it to you
> 3. APPEARANCE - Thank God for looking good, Aknowledge & Compliment others, All things come from...
> 4. KNOWLEDGE - Let others talk, let them express their own, Encourage them, Build up their self confid...
> 5. ACHIEVEMENT - Magnify others in your success, ... others & share it w. them
> 6. GIFTS AND TALENTS - people act as if they got their g... on there own, (God gives all gifts)
> 7. 2 Cor. 12:7 - God gives pain to keep us from being Prideful

LOCKED IN ADDICTION

INTRAMURAL CORRESPONDENCE
4835-3105
CSJ-105 12/96

Name: Tongue   No.:   Date: 3-20-2001
Assignment: Our Words   Lock:

PHILL 4:13 I HAVE THE STRENGTH FOR EVERYTHING THROUGH HIM WHO STRENGTHENS ME (OR) I CAN DO ALL THINGS IN CHRIST THAT WHO STRENGTHEN ME

PROV 18:21 DEATH & LIFE ARE IN THE POWER OF THE TONGUE,
PROV 18:4 THE WORDS FROM A MAN'S MOUTH ARE DEEP WATERS.
HEB 5:12 THE WORD OF GOD IS SHARPER THAN ANY TWO EDGED SWORD, PENETRATING BETWEEN SOUL & SPIRIT, JOINTS & MARROW, AND ABLE TO DISCERN REFLECTIONS & THOUGHTS OF THE HEART

SPIRIT IS IN US.   SPIRIT HAS MANY GIFTS   CORIN 12:4
FRUITS OF SPIRIT GAL. 5:22

BY THESE GIFTS WE CAN DO ALL THINGS

PHILLIP 1:1   TO THE SAINT (HOLY ONES)

FR ROBERT FOX
(CHAPEL ANNAISE) DAMASCUS SYRIA
MORNA - NICHOLAS NAZOR Nov. 27, 1982
HE WHO HAS DIVIDED THE CHURCH SINS
SUFFERING FACE OF JESUS CHRIST
THE VIRGIN HOME   (MORNA, HAS THE STIGMATAS
(LADY OF SOFANIA)

FREEDOM BEHIND BARS

I continued to sleep with my dream journal next to my bed; I would write about Bible verses and what was happening in prison. I kept so many of my notes from that time.

Even though I was finding my way through Christ, the conversion didn't completely change me. I didn't wake up one day a Harvard scholar. I still had the street talk going on, and still do today.

I wrote a note that said something along these lines. "Listen, chaplain, don't play with me," I said. "Either I will sue you or I will sue the institution, or both. You don't know me. My family is capable of doing it, so you better get me Catholic service or put me on a bus and ride me out of here."

The City Lion

Although I was being transformed, I still had this street-like mentality in me.

I was redirecting any anger that lingered about being in prison to my passion for the faith. All I kept thinking about was that number 11, and I was determined to get the men I needed to commit to go to Catholic service.

I shared a cell with a guy named Gary who slept on the bunk above me. I asked him to come to Catholic service, but he quickly responded that he wasn't interested. He asked me if I was Chaldean and I explained that I was Chaldean and I shared with him my family background. We realized his sister was married to my relative. At first, he didn't believe me, but then he was convinced I was telling the truth.

"Come on, Gary — come to service with us," I said.

"No, man, I told you that I am not into that Jesus stuff," he responded.

"Come on. I will help you, Gary."

"No."

"Okay, man, I will be there for you."

That morning, I woke up at 3 a.m. and felt this burning fire in my heart. I wanted to get this service going. I saw Gary's eyes open, blood red. He was tired but couldn't sleep. Inmate McDonald was snoring like a tank. I was sleeping across the cell on a lower bunk.

I looked at Gary. "What if I can make McDonald stop snoring?" I asked. "Will you come to service?"

"You are going to make him stop snoring? I am going to kill this guy."

"If you kill him, you will end up in the hole, but if I make him stop snoring, then you come to Catholic service."

"What? Okay, I got to see this."

"You got to see this, alright. I do this, you got to come to Catholic service. If you don't come, I will beat you down, Gary. You are telling me you're going to come. You better come."

"Okay, man. I will come."

I raised my hand over McDonald and shouted, "In the name of Jesus, I command you to stop snoring!"

Gary looked at me with the same crazy look so many people had when they saw me praying on people. He was annoyed.

I said it again. Then I shouted louder: "In the name of Jesus, I command you to stop snoring NOW!"

Just like that, McDonald stopped snoring. I looked over at Gary.

"You are coming to Catholic service, man."

It was 4 in the morning. I grabbed the sheet for Gary to sign, committing him to go to Catholic service — and he kept his commitment. He came every week. McDonald, who stood 6 feet 3 inches tall and weighed at least 285 pounds, never snored again.

I started Catholic service March 10, 2000. I couldn't get a priest, so I started preaching every week. At my first service, I read John 4 about the Samaritan woman. All I had was a Catholic Bible with directions in the back on how to read the Bible and preach about it. I bought a Catholic study Bible. It was the best $50 I ever spent. Every week I felt the Holy Spirit directing me how to preach.

By Thursday of every week, the Lord spoke to me, and I knew what I should talk about during service. I began writing many notes. We had these long sheets of paper in prison.

Sometimes I would grab napkins, or whatever I could find, and write verses on them. I often look at my old notes and read the Scripture on them. I love reading those notes because they remind me where I came from and that I'm so happy with who I am today.

I preached without a priest for five years in that prison. Even on the rare occasion that a priest would come, they still let me preach. One priest always told me it was a calling, and he stood by as I talked about the Scripture. At one point, a priest named Father Jewel came to the prison. When he first heard about me preaching, he asked an inmate, Matthew, if I always preached like that, to

LOCKED IN ADDICTION

which he replied, "Yes sir, every week. He is on fire for Jesus."

The priest approached me.

"Son, who brings all these men in here?"

"Jesus," I replied.

"Yes, of course; but who is in charge?" he asked.

"I am."

He started to hear confession. He then turned to me.

"Son, I've got to tell you something. I go to prison, and I get 10, 20 men — tops — who come to church. You've got up to 50 men here every week. This is your service. This is not mine."

"Come on, Father. Don't play with me."

"Nope. This is your calling. It is not my calling. I will come here every four months and hear confession, but this is your service."

"Father Jewel, please. I have been waiting more than two years for a priest. I have written every diocese — Saginaw, Detroit, and Grand Rapids. I have been waiting for you."

"No. I am not going to come every week. This is your calling. You do it."

The priest would not come every week. So, I continued on my own.

A call to serve

Men started coming to me — men I did not know and who were from various religions. A Muslim man approached me one day and said that God came to him in a dream and told him to find me in the prison.

Another day it was a Protestant and then a Jewish man. Men searched me out, asking me to share with them what I knew about Jesus. I carried on for five years, preaching and teaching inside the prison walls just as I was learning. I read Scripture every day. At one point, I began ministering to the officers, even the ones who antagonized me.

Daily and for months, Officer Scott intentionally walked by me and said the same thing: "Naemi, you are never going home."

I would respond with the same answer: "Satan, when the Lord says it is time, these doors will open."

Every day it continued. Officer Scott would try different approaches to trigger the anger that once lived inside me.

"Naemi, no man stays in prison 20 years and makes it out in the world," he said.

"Shut up, Satan," I replied. "I will pay more in taxes than you make in salary."

When I did eventually get out, I started my own produce distribution company where I sold fruits and vegetables to stores and I did pay more in taxes than he made. I am not mentioning this as a sting to him or to brag. I had such faith in God that I knew it would be true.

I really cared about Officer Scott. He had been married to a pastor's daughter who left him, and he started to hate Christians. I tried to comfort him and tell him the sun would shine again one day and that a good woman was waiting for him.

"Shut up, you hypocrite," he would often reply.

"It is okay. The church is filled with hypocrites," I said. "It doesn't mean the word of God is not truth."

I never gave up. I kept telling him that his life would turn around and that he needed to have faith. Eventually it did. Officer Scott met another woman and got remarried.

Then there was Officer Newville and his family. I talked to him about Jesus every day, and Officer McDonald and I became friends.

One morning, I was talking with several officers. It was as if I was no longer a prisoner, but a buddy to them all.

Officer Lot was living with a girl and confessed he was afraid to marry her. Like buddies often do, I would use every moment to rile him.

"Hey Officer Lot, how is that hooker you are living with?"

"Naemi, if you don't shut up, I will beat you up."

"You can't beat up anyone. Try. I will beat you down."

"Naemi, stop talking about my girl."

"She ain't your girl. If she was your girl, you would have married her. She is not a girl. She is your prostitute; that is why you don't want to marry her."

Nothing was sugar coated in prison. I spoke street slang and engaged in some crude conversations. I learned to tame it and not use cuss words, but I had to figure out how to still fit in and be taken seriously while inside. There was no such thing as being polite or politically correct in prison. It was harsh and "in your face."

I wouldn't quit antagonizing Officer Lot until he married his girlfriend. I knew she was a good woman but wanted him to realize that living with her was not right. He needed to do the respectful thing and marry her.

FREEDOM BEHIND BARS

A time for prayer

During my days at Pine River, I would wake up at 5 a.m. Prisoners were not allowed to go into the activity room until 6. I went in anyway. I wanted privacy to pray with Jesus. An officer came up to me the first morning.

"Hey, what are you doing in here? You are not allowed in here," said Officer Cheney.

I looked at him and pulled out my identification card. "Yes, sir; here is my ID. Write me up a violation."

The officer looked confusingly at me. I knew he was thinking, "This guy wants a violation?" and I was prepared to say that I didn't care. He looked at me again with narrowed eyes and a stern look.

"Here is your ID?" he retorted sarcastically. "Write me up?"

I could hear the irritation in his voice.

"Yes, sir. Here is my ID. Write me up."

"You want a violation?"

"I don't care. I will stay indoors. Jesus is more important than going outside."

The next day, I went into the activity room and there was Officer Cheney.

"Didn't I tell you yesterday not to come in here before 6?" he asked.

"Yes, sir. Don't mean to be disrespectful, sir, but here is my ID. You can write me up."

LOCKED IN ADDICTION

So, he wrote me up.

The third morning he came up to me again.

"Didn't I tell you that you cannot be here?"

"Yes, sir. You can write me up."

"You take this stuff pretty seriously, don't you?"

"Yes, sir, I do."

"Okay."

He walked back inside his office, and I stood watching as he ripped up the violation. If it had been submitted, I would have been locked inside the building for days. I would not be able to go to the yard or weight pit. Every morning I continued to wake up at 5 in the morning to be with Jesus.

And they called me "Brother" Tom

As my prayer life became stronger, the prisoners started to call me "Brother" Tom.

As a speaker, I'm usually asked several questions during my talks. An event from my time prison often comes to mind as I engage in conversation.

"When did they start calling you Brother Tom?" That was one question that led me to a memory I hadn't thought about in a while. It was 2002. I was at the Pine River prison when the ministry grew. Carrie was a prison volunteer and used to deliver the Eucharist to inmates who were Catholic. She told me one day that she would no longer be able to come to the prison. I thought they revoked her visitation rights. She said, "Tom, I am getting old. I got boils on my legs and I don't feel good."

As soon as she said that I began to feel an intense heat from the Holy Spirit rise within me. "Don't you know the devil is a liar?" I asked in anger. "You are the servant of the Lord, and the devil is trying to trick you, so you don't come here and bless these men. Let me lay hands on these legs."

Without waiting for a response from Carrie, I laid my hands on her legs and began to pray. She was shocked. She hadn't seen me pray over anyone, although she heard about it from some of the prisoners.

Two weeks later, Carrie walked into the prison shouting that she had been healed. When I first met her, she was already in her mid- to late 70s. After I prayed on her, she continued to bring the Eucharist and go to the prison. Even three or four years after I left Pine River, I heard Carrie was still volunteering.

Wally was another prison volunteer. He and Carrie would rotate weeks bringing us the Eucharist. He had gray hair, stood about 6'1" and was in his mid-50s. One day he walked into the prison crying and I asked him what was wrong. He told me about his grandson who couldn't speak. He had autism. The Lord put on my heart that the boy would speak. "Wally, in four months, your grandson will speak," I said. Four months later, he did just that — he spoke, just like the Lord said he would.

A couple of years later, Wally walked into the prison and said, "Boys, I want you all to pray for my father." He told us that his father had water on his heart. I was folding sheets one afternoon when Wally stepped out of the room. I was not permitted to follow. As Wally stepped out, I heard the Lord say to me, *"Tom, you can't go to his dad, but you can lay hands on Wally, and he can go to his dad."*

LOCKED IN ADDICTION

As soon as I heard those words, I ran to the edge of the door and yelled to Wally, "Come back, Wally! Come back!"

"What is it, Brother Tom?" he asked.

"The Lord spoke to me. He said that I cannot lay hands on your dad, but you can. So, go straight to the hospital and lay hands on your dad, and this is what you are going to say: 'By the stripes of Jesus you are healed.'"

"Okay, Brother Tom, I believe you."

Wally sat on a stool and as soon as I laid hands on him, I could hear the wind of the Holy Spirit, the buzz and the sound of a windstorm. My body temperature began to rise.

"Wally, can you hear the Holy Spirit? Can you feel it?"

"No, Brother Tom, but I believe you."

In that instant I began to pray silently, "Lord, I don't know how this man is not feeling the Holy Spirit, because I feel it."

I screamed, "In the name of Jesus," and as soon as I spoke those words, Wally's mouth broke loose. He began to speak in tongues like a madman, and it seemed as though he was speaking a million words a minute.

"Oh, you don't feel it, huh?" I asked.

Wally came back the next Sunday and asked the prisoners, "You know where my dad is?"

Everyone wanted to know.

"My dad went to Orlando, Florida. Brother Tom told me to go lay hands on him Sunday and he left the hospital on Monday morning."

Those years at Pine River were significant preaching years for me. One morning, I felt the Word speaking to me: *"Submit yourself to God. Resist the devil. He will be free from you. Draw near to God and he will draw near to you. Cleanse your hands, you sinners; purify your heart."*

I knew God was telling me to read James 4:7-8, but I had no idea why. I started talking to God.

"Okay, God, I am reading this, but who is this for?"

After I finished praying, I started to prepare my usual morning breakfast — the same one I had been eating for the last 10 years. We had two units back-to-back and the officers changed over during lunch and breakfast. There were four offices — two at each unit. There was a door between the units, but no one could open the door except an officer. Someone left a Bible on the microwave. I grabbed it. It was open to James 4.

"Okay, Lord," I prayed, "You spoke this Bible verse to me this morning and now there is a Bible here open to the same chapter. What are you trying to tell me? Who is this for, Jesus?"

The door opened and there stood Officer Finley, with the saddest look on his face.

"Officer Finley, what's wrong?"

The officer began to weep. "Tom, my son committed suicide yesterday."

At that moment, I knew why the Lord had been giving me those words from James. Here was Officer Finley in deep despair. I now knew what it meant.

"Submit yourself to the Lord," I told him. "I know what I am saying sounds crazy, but you have to trust the Lord on this one."

I walked into the office with him, and he knew that those words were for him. I sat there and prayed with him and for him. I began to realize that so many officers were just as tormented as the prisoners. I knew that God was calling me to evangelize to both.

I hated evil and I hated the devil. Inside prison was this large man plastered with tattoos. I wanted to fight this guy. I could feel the rage every time he was near me. During my workouts, I would cut in and say, "Hey, man, move over." While we were pumping iron, he never wanted to look me in the eyes. I was purposely trying to get to him to fight.

Ricky, a friend of mine, would sit outside the cell smoking with Brother Sal, a preacher who killed his wife. I would go out there and shout the Word because I knew these guys in F block were devil worshipers. "When the King of Glory comes, He is going to mop up all of these cowards," I'd yell.

Ricky would beg me to stop, but his pleading just ignited my spirit more.

"My God is the King of Kings and every knee will bow in His presence."

I would see these guys trembling. Every day I stood in front of them and preached about God and against the devil. Not once did they look my way.

"Coward Satan!" I shouted and spat on the floor.

Brother Sal came up to me one day and said, "I tell you, Brother Tom — I have never seen a preacher like you before."

He told me that he had a vision of killing his wife. He started doing drugs. Money came in from preaching, and he fooled around with women. The devil is smart. He knows how to work on someone. He entices people, and that is exactly what happened with Brother Sal.

Delivering Daniel

As much as I wanted out of prison, I knew I would never leave until I did one last thing. Inside at the end of my time in prison, it was all about delivering a man named Daniel. Every time I tell this story to someone who now knows me and knows about my ministry, it is no longer a complete shock to that person. They don't give me the look of disbelief. With those people, I usually end up laughing and sometimes crying with them. The story does provoke various emotions.

It is a typical response from friends I've made at the Eastern Catholic Re-Evangelization Center or at churches—those who have heard my testimony. Often, I share something they haven't heard before about my life in prison. There are things I have forgotten about until a particular question or conversation triggers a memory. Even while writing this book, stories I buried deep inside my soul began to surface. I was being set free from my own bondage through the prayers of others—but I wouldn't find complete freedom until I delivered Daniel.

Officer Daniel sought me out. He would see me reading Scripture and always ask what I was reading. I answered the same way every time.

"You know what I am reading. I am reading the word of salvation. I am reading the word of eternal life. You need to come and know it because you know you need to be saved."

LOCKED IN ADDICTION

"Oh, Tom, I am not with that Christian stuff," he would say.

"You are not with that Christian stuff, but you are with that devil stuff," I would answer.

Officer Daniel always started the conversation but would walk away once I began to reply. I played along and continued this daily dialogue, knowing there was a reason Officer Daniel questioned me every day. I was scheduled to be released in 2000. In May of that year, I was called into the counselor's office. There sat a man, a counselor and officer across from me.

"Mr. Naemi, it has been nice meeting you," he said. "You have been an ideal prisoner. You have been approved to leave. You are going to be on the bus Tuesday morning for the center action."

This is when you go home, but you are still under state restrictions. You must report back at night to a state-run facility, but I would be free to work during the day. This meant that I would have been sent to a halfway house. I would be monitored for two years. I would work during the day and be ordered home at night. The Thursday before that day, I saw a prisoner I had never met named Jim. He told me he had two dreams about me—two times, back-to-back. He said it was about two of my countrymen, even though he didn't know where I was from. There were two dark-looking guys with an American guy, and one was smoking a cigarette. He told me, "One said to the other about you, 'This guy cannot get out, because we are going to kill him or keep him in prison.'"

"Don't worry about me, brother," I said. "I am going to be just fine. Whoever goes against me, the mighty hand of God will fall on him like an ax."

FREEDOM BEHIND BARS

The following Tuesday I was supposed to get on the bus, so I started to pack. I gave away some books and clothes to the other inmates.

The previous morning, I got word that someone called the prosecutor's office and the prison board telling them not to let me out. The prosecutor wrote a letter as if I was some organized criminal. The letter said not to release me because I had connections in Iraq and Mexico, and I would kill people.

That Monday morning, I heard the counselor call my name on the overhead speaker: "Naemi to the office."

I walked in and there the counselor and the officer sat.

"Something is going on, Naemi. Someone called Lansing. They stopped you from leaving tomorrow."

"What are you talking about?" I asked. "I was approved."

"Yeah, we know, but you have been unapproved. Someone is working against you."

I called my family. They called my attorney and I called Lansing. No one in Lansing called back. Then it occurred to me maybe I wasn't ready to go home because I needed to know more. I needed to do more.

However, when I finally got out of prison I bumped into that prosecutor, who was now serving in another political capacity. A friend walked me up to him at a country club and introduced me to him as the man he helped keep in prison longer than he should have been there. I don't believe in revenge, but my friend thought it was necessary. In 2002, I was eligible for a meeting with the parole board. I could hear the words of St. Paul loudly in my ear: "Be imitators of me as I am in Christ" (I Corinthians 11:1).

I began to talk to God. "Okay, Lord, I am not going home. I am going to be here for a while because you have work for me to do."

I stood up after that parole board meeting and shouted to the prisoners, "Guys, I am not going home. I got bad news on the way."

Not even 20 minutes later, Officer Newville approached me.

"You got hammered, Naemi."

"How so?"

"You got 18 more."

"Eighteen more years?" I replied sarcastically.

"No, 18 more months, man."

"It is only for the glory of God because I have work to do here."

I was not yet free, but I was maturing in my faith. It had been almost two years since I started preaching and evangelizing. At this point, I had seen all kinds of people in prison get healed.

I knew that my faith had taken a giant leap. And I knew that I would never be released until Officer Daniel was delivered to Jesus. I went to another parole board meeting and, once again, I sat across from the board and immediately sensed something was wrong.

"Thank you, Mr. Naemi, for the interview," a woman said while she pointed at my file.

"Is there something in my file?" I asked.

"Have a good day, Mr. Naemi. Thank you very much for your time," she said, almost shouting.

I walked out and called my attorney.

"There was something in my file at the parole board meeting. Find out what it is, and we must take them to court."

Although I wanted to know what was going on, I knew it was not about the parole board or anyone else. It was God's timing. More time passed and I was no closer to finding out what was in my file. It was now May 2003, and I was reading Psalms: "I will call upon God and the Lord will save me at dusk, dawn and noon … I will grieve and complain and my prayer will be heard, and God will give me freedom and peace from those who are against me … there are many opposed to me … cast your care upon the Lord" (Psalms 55:17-19).

I kissed the Bible and said, "This is beautiful."

I kept reading and it seemed liked the Word jumped out of the Bible. I could see these 4-foot-wide letters floating on the air in front of me. I was amazed by the image. It was May 25, 2003. I wrote in my Bible, "This is for me. This is freedom for me."

I knew the Lord was preparing for my freedom, although God's timing took two-and-a-half more years. One day I was leading a service and only 17 men showed up. I was shocked and began to wonder if I was doing something wrong. I thought maybe I upset the Lord. I left the service and walked to a small yard.

"Lord the last thing I want to do is upset you," I prayed. "If I am not preaching correctly, I'm going to stop doing what I'm doing."

I asked the volunteers to pray for me and I asked the Holy Spirit to guide them to pray for me.

The chaplain's clerk was my friend and an ex-Marine. "Every request we opened up was a request for a Catholic Church," he

LOCKED IN ADDICTION

said. "I told the Chaplain that Naemi boy was working hard recruiting people to his church."

"No, it's not Naemi; it is Jesus," I replied.

"You gotta be kidding me," he said.

That Tuesday I had a dream. The prisoners and I were in a gym, sitting in the shape of a triangle. A prisoner named Fox was sitting in the front row. The gym was packed. I heard the Lord say, *"Tom, I want you to teach them. Tom, I want you to teach them. Teach them, Tom."*

When God gives you a word, you are going to get confirmation. The Lord always speaks in threes.

I woke up and wrote, "The Lord wants me to teach them. I see the men sitting in the gym."

That Sunday I headed to service and had 58 men with me. The officer said, "Where are you going?"

"We are going to service."

"Are you kidding me, man? You're going to have nearly 60 men in that room? You are going to be like sardines."

"Look, man — we are going in there and we are going to praise God, no matter where we are."

The officer picked up the phone and called the control center.

"There are too many men for this room," he said. "There are almost 60 men; the room is too small."

He was told to put us in the gym. As I preached, I remembered the dream from four days earlier. That following Monday, I received a letter from Dennis, another inmate from Lapeer. Michelle, one of the volunteers, was driving when she had a vision to pray for me. He told me in the letter that they were all praying for me. I knew they were praying for this prison ministry. I took it as a sign they were praying for me to reach more men.

I understood that sometimes God puts you in one place to help deliver a soul to Christ, and I knew that Officer Daniel's soul had to get delivered. He had a wife and four kids, and God loved him like he loved all His children. I was thinking about all of this and then looked up — and there stood Officer Daniel.

"How long are you going to keep screwing around and running away from God?" I asked him. Daniel was an officer and I shouted at him like he was a kid. Every time I talked to him about God, he ran away. A couple of hours went by, and I was back to reading the Bible. Officer Daniel began to walk closer to me.

"What are you reading?" he asked.

"You know what I am reading," I shouted. "You know you need salvation. Stop screwing around."

Days continued to pass and finally Officer Daniel was receptive. He asked me to come to his office. At 7 at night, when most prisoners went to the yard, I went to his office.

"I need help, Tom," he said.

"What help do you need, Officer Daniel?"

"That devil worshiper from earlier who was big with tattoos put a hex on me."

"He is a coward and the one he worships is a coward," I said. "When they break yard at 7, call me in the office. You need to give your life to Jesus."

"I have a problem with porn," he said.

Officer McDonald had gone on break, so I knew this was a good time to grab my Bible. I opened it to Luke 9.

"See what Luke said, Officer Daniel? He said we have power and authority in the name of Jesus," I explained.

I put my hand on his forehead and shouted, "I have power and authority in the name of Jesus and in the power of the Holy Spirit."

The wind of the Holy Spirit came at that moment. The spirit was buzzing. My body temperature rose. I was burning up. While praying on him, Officer Daniel fell to his knees. His cap fell off and he fell backwards. He was crying and I was rebuking the devil and every evil spirit that came upon his family. I rebuked that spirit of pornography and the evil spirit of lust.

Then Officer McDonald walked in and saw me praying and Officer Daniel on his knees, crying. He walked away. He was a Christian man and he knew if he reported us, Officer Daniel would lose his job and I would be sent to the hole.

"Now I can go home," I said.

"Shut up, Naemi; you are not here because of me."

"Yes, I have been here for five years for you. I knew that once you came to Jesus, I could go home."

A week or two passed. Officer Daniel came in at shift change. I knew he was remorseful, but he was not going to church. With my Bible in hand, I was determined to fully deliver this man to Jesus.

"Hi, Naemi," shouted Officer Daniel.

"What is this I hear?" I asked. "You are remorseful, but you are not going to church?"

He ran from me, but he returned. He grabbed my arm.

"How do you know these things?"

"I have a crystal ball under my bed," I joked. "How do you think I know these things?"

"Man, I need to talk to you," he said.

"Yeah? Talk to me."

"When you prayed on me that day, I was on fire for three days. I couldn't sleep. I made my wife get rid of all the porn. We threw out all the dirty magazines. We threw out all the dirty videos. I took my kids and went to the first church I saw. When the pastor asked if anyone had a testimony, I raised my hand. I told them how I got delivered. The pastor was amazed that there was an inmate who could pray like you do, but as soon as I told him you were Catholic, he took the microphone from my hands. Everyone gave me the cold shoulder."

I laughed.

"You know why, Daniel?" I asked.

"Why?"

"Because some Protestants don't think Catholics know the Holy Spirit. What were you born?"

"I was born Lutheran," he answered.

"I don't care what church you go to, but if you don't get Je-

LOCKED IN ADDICTION

sus in your life, I am never going home."

"Cut it out, Naemi. I am not the reason you are still in prison."

"How many times do I have to tell you? The minute you get delivered is the minute I get to go home."

The following day, I headed to Bible study. There were about 20 to 25 men there. Officer Daniel was off this day. I stood up and told the men that they needed to pray for him.

While they prayed, Officer Daniel was in his car. He heard a voice in his head: "Turn left. Turn left. Turn left. Then, turn here and turn here."

His car pulled up in the parking lot of a Lutheran church. He ran into the prison the next day looking for me. "Tom, you are never going to believe what happened to me yesterday," he said.

"What happened?" I asked.

"I was driving and this voice ..." he said, as he continued to tell the story.

"What time was this?" I asked.

"It was around 2 o'clock."

"We were praying for you. We had Bible study at the time."

"That explains why. I could hear a voice telling me where to turn."

"That is why. Get your butt into church," I said. He started going to church. He came into prison and told me that he had a dream that I packed up and went home. The next time I went to the parole board, my cousin Jimmy was with me and he was prepared to talk, but the parole board didn't give him a chance. In fact, one man on the board just shouted at him.

FREEDOM BEHIND BARS

"I don't care what you have to say," he said to Jimmy. "Get out of here, both of you."

We walked out. Jimmy looked at me. "Man, how do you talk to these people?"

"You don't. You sit and you listen. They do all the talking."

Although still part of the prison system, I was transferred to the state facility in Coldwater Michigan. While there, I heard my cousins — brothers Jimmy and Steve — bumped into the governor of Michigan, at a party - whom they knew well.

They told her my story, that I had been in prison for nearly 15 years and that there was no need for the state to keep me inside. I was not a threat to anyone, they said.

The governor asked about my history. They told her that there were people working against me to keep me in prison. I later heard she sent a letter to the parole board asking why I was still locked up. This is, of course, what people told me. I never personally ever talked to her. I truly believe that if the letter was sent, it made all the affect in the world – probably the reason I got out.

I was taken to the Coldwater prison Monday, March 10, 2005—five years from the day I entered Pine River. I felt the Lord saying to me, *"No matter where you go, I will always be with you."*

This prison is on the border with Indiana. I never knew why I was sent there, but I had my suspicions. At the first service I attended at the Coldwater prison, I met a deacon, a priest, and a volunteer. There were only nine inmates at the service.

"What is going on here? Why are there only nine inmates?"

I asked.

"You know, Tom, the men don't like to come," one of them said.

I started going to the yard and preaching. Before you know it, I had nearly 40 men in the first month. They continued to come every week. One of the inmates had diabetes and wouldn't come to church.

"Where are you going, Wygall?" I shouted at him.

"Tom, I have diabetes bad and I have to go to the health clinic to check my blood," he said.

"Come here, Wygall. You don't need health care; you need Jesus."

"I know Tom, but I need health care, too."

I laid hands on him and shouted, "In the name of Jesus, I command healing upon you."

He went to his appointment the next day and his blood sugar was normal. It was the same story on the second and third days. "Tom, this is crazy," said Wygall. "I have never gone three days without insulin."

"Well, you are done," I said.

"No, Tom, I have been diabetic for nine years."

"I don't care how long it has been; you are healed."

He had his blood tested for several more days, and still no insulin was needed. "How long are you going to keep going?" I laughed. "Sunday we are going to put this to rest. Everyone is going to give me their pudding if I am right."

I handed Wygall a pile of about 30 pudding cups.

"Either this will kill me or I am healed," he said as he started to eat.

He headed back to the health clinic the next day and there was no difference. He walked into church shouting, "I want to give God the glory! I had diabetes for nine years. I have gone to health care every day for 14 days and I still don't need insulin. I am healed."

Harry, a volunteer, asked him who had prayed on him. I told him not to tell him.

"Brother Tom," he said.

"Well, preaching is not my only gift," I told Harry.

David Wygall brought me a guy named Todd. He had hunchback and brittle bone disease. "Tom, this guy wants to go to church," said David. "No, he is not going to church," I said. "He has regular sex with men. I don't want to disturb church. It is holy place."

I started to walk away and David grabbed my arms. I could see from the look in David's eyes that he was sincere. I looked at Todd.

"Listen, Todd — I will let you come to church, but if you do anything unclean or ungodly in church, I will rip your head off. I will beat you down like you have never been beaten down before."

I was still in prison, and when in "Rome," you must do what they do. I had to get through to these guys by speaking their language. I let them know I meant business. I know it sounds crazy, but I actually had to still beat up guys every once in a while, to prove I was strong.

LOCKED IN ADDICTION

I prayed for Todd in the yard that day.

When I was out in the yard talking to some other prisoners one day, Todd came up to me and told me that ever since I prayed on him, he no longer had pain in his body.

"Praise the Lord," I said.

"Praise the Lord; amen to that," said Todd.

Days later he came up to me again.

"Tom, I went to health care today, but I told them that I didn't need medication because Jesus has healed me."

"Glory to God," I said. "That is a big step."

"Yeah, I have not taken a pill for four weeks."

Before I went home, Todd stood taller, and his back straightened out.

One day during service, Harry started preaching some off-the-wall crap that everyone and every religion is going to go to Heaven. "Slow up, Harry," I interrupted. "Not everyone is going to Heaven. Not all Christians are going to Heaven if they are not living a Christian life. Read the Bible. Stop saying that."

"Oh, Tom, you don't understand the Catholic way," he said.

"What are you talking about? I understand the Catholic teachings. Not everyone is going to Heaven. I understand it well."

"Do you know what the catechism says?"

"Yeah, I know the catechism and it says that Jesus died for the sins of all mankind. Those who do not know Jesus fall under the blood of Jesus, but those who do know will be judge severely. If what you are saying is true, then Jesus did not have to die. The whole objective of being Christian is save people to come to Christ."

Harry did it again the following Sunday. I told him again that he had to stop and that he was turning off the crowd. The men did not want to hear this untruth. The third week, he did it again. I went crazy.

"You stupid idiot!" I shouted. "How many times have I told you to get your stuff right? Don't teach any bad theology here."

Officers came in and handcuffed me and took me to the control center, but luckily the man in charge was Catholic.

"What is going on, Naemi?" he said. "I heard you were threatening a volunteer?"

"No, sir, I was not threatening a volunteer," I said. "I am just telling him about Jesus, but he is giving them bad messages. I have been working hard to bring these men to Jesus and he is ruining everything."

"We have a situation on our hands. Either we write you up, you sign off from the Catholic service or we ship you out."

"Ship me out. I will go to another prison."

"Listen, make it easier and just sign off from the Catholic service. This way he won't say you threatened him."

"Okay, I will sign off and I will not go to Catholic service."

I started preaching in the yard, but the rule was you could only have six men gathered at one time. I created groups of six, with me in the center. I preached every day for up to two hours a day. The officers loved it. They stood and listened and would ask me questions.

LOCKED IN ADDICTION

One day I got these words of knowledge. They just came to me. I saw a group of non-believers. I was preaching about Jesus. I got into it with these non-believers and they cuffed me and sent me back to the same Catholic guard.

"Naemi, what are you doing? Are you trying to start a riot?" he asked.

"No, I am trying to bring people to Jesus," I said.

"Listen, you are up for parole soon. If you don't stop this, we will yank your parole."

I agreed to stop getting into people's faces. I realized they sent me to the Coldwater prison for those last few months to evaluate my state of mind — to see if I was crazy or out to get anyone, which I was not.

"No more preaching in the yard," he said.

"Okay, no problem," I replied.

I started preaching and leading Bible studies in the unit.

One day there were about 160 men in there. I went to get my clothes out of my locker, and I got this whirlwind of inspiration to preach about Jesus. I began to shout:

"I yelled out when the trumpet blows, and the kingdom of Heaven comes with an army of white horses. There is going to be war on this evil. No one knows His name because His name is King of Kings. He declares war on the evil. All these demons in here will go into the lake of fire."

I felt like I was preaching and going crazy at the same time.

FREEDOM BEHIND BARS

I knew two guys by the name of Big Red in prison, one in Jackson and one in Coldwater. They were both big, tall guys with red hair.

Big Red stood up and said, "Brother Tom, the devil had no say in that matter."

"You sympathize with the devil," I said as my voice got louder. "You can go to hell with the devil."

He got quiet. No one wanted to fight me.

The day after I had this preaching outbreak, Big Red came to me crying.

"Please, Naemi; I don't want to go to hell with the devil."

"Yeah. You are right."

I prayed with him in the morning and lead him to Christ.

In the summer of 2005, I was sitting at a lunch table with three other men. On my right side was an atheist, on my left an older Protestant and in front of me was another Protestant. All of the sudden I heard the Lord's voice say to me, *"If the people would heed my voice they would turn from their wicked ways, humble themselves and turn to me, I will heal their land."*

I heard His voice say the same thing twice more.

"Okay, Lord, what are you saying? Who is that for?" I asked.

The atheist asked, "Oh, God is speaking to you?"

"Yeah; as a matter of fact, God speaks all the time," I said.

"He does?"

LOCKED IN ADDICTION

"Yeah, he does; you just have to listen carefully."

The older Protestant prisoner asked what I was saying and what it meant.

"Something is going to happen very soon and very bad, and that is a warning," I said.

The next day, Hurricane Katrina hit New Orleans.

A reflection on being locked in the prison cell of addiction

In 2018, it was reported that legendary rock star Alice Cooper credited his faith in Jesus for helping him beat his addiction to alcohol and turn his life around. In an interview with *New York Daily News' Confidential,* Cooper said, "Everything that could go wrong was shutting down inside of me ... I was drinking with Jim Morrison and Jimi Hendrix and trying to keep up with Keith Moon, and they all died at 27."

Cooper thought he was going to die, and, like Officer Daniel, he needed to be delivered. He went back to his Christian roots and rediscovered Jesus. He needed to connect to Christ to be released from porn. That connection to our Lord is the virtue we need to be free from the vice of addiction.

He and his wife are both Christians. His father was a pastor and his grandfather an evangelist. He grew up in the church yet strayed far away from it; came close to death and then returned.

Since being released from prison, I have come across hundreds of people addicted to one thing or another. I have traveled to different states and countries as part of my prayer ministry, and everywhere I go there are people trapped inside an addiction – sex, porn, drugs, food, shopping, alcohol, work, violence, tobacco, exer-

FREEDOM BEHIND BARS

cise, gossip - the list can go on. I always ask people when they share these addiction stories about their prayer life. It all starts with pray if you haven't figured that out yet. It is about surrendering to God as you have read scripture. I did just that to release myself from the wickedness that imprisoned me for so many years.

It is by living the virtues that release us from the vices. We can look to the virtue of temperance when we are trying to work through addictions. There are all kinds of addictions to substances, to food, to shopping, to sex, to pornography, and the list goes on. With the virtue of temperance, we are asked to analyze our lives and be specific areas such as self-control, setting goals to accomplish, staying accountable, reviewing our progress, denying ourselves in ways of engaging in fasting.

Temperance can be defined as showing restraint in eating or drinking, and especially avoiding alcohol. An example of temperance is when you refrain from drinking any alcohol. I am not saying don't seek medical help for addictions, of course, go get help form professionals, but ultimate healing is found in Christ. We also need spiritual healing from our addictions. There are 12-step programs that have helped tens of thousands of people with addictions such as alcoholism. In those 12-step programs, there is a focus on a greater power. Of course, as Christians, we know that greater power to be God and our Lord and Savior Jesus Christ.

Do you find yourself in these scenarios that could be an addiction?

- You have lost all control over yourself.
- You can't seem to live without doing or having that particular thing.
- You are anxious, stressed or even angry when you can't have that thing you are addicted to.

LOCKED IN ADDICTION

- Whatever it is, it consumed your every thought.
- You know you need help.

Reflective Questions

1. What are you addicted to?
2. What led to the addiction?
3. What have you done to release yourself from the addiction?
4. What else can you do?
5. How can you incorporate the virtue of temperance into your life?

If you are locked in addiction of sin, here are some Bible verses to meditate on:

"So, if a son frees you, then you will truly be free" (John 8:36)

"He summoned the Twelve and gave them power and authority over all demons and to cure diseases, and he sent them to proclaim the kingdom of God and to heal (the sick)" (Luke 9:1-2).

"My message and my proclamation were not with persuasive (words of) wisdom, but with a demonstration of spirit and power, so that your faith might rest not on human wisdom but on the power of God" (1 Corinthians 2:4-5).

"Do not give what is holy to dogs, or throw your

FREEDOM BEHIND BARS

pearls before swine, lest they trample them underfoot, and turn and tear you to pieces" (Matthew 7:6).

"When they hand you over, do not worry about how you are to speak or what you are to say. You will be given at that moment what you are to say. For it will not be you who speaks but the Spirit of your Father speaking through you" (Matthew 10:19-20).

"Do not conform yourselves to this age but be transformed by the renewal of your mind, that you may discern what is the will of God, what is good and pleasing and perfect" (Romans 12:2).

Chapter 9

FINALLY, FREE

"Peter said repent and be baptized and the gifts will be given to you and your family" -Acts 2:38.

I was finally going home. I found real freedom six years earlier in Christ, but I was now free to live outside prison walls.

More than 10 people arrived in a stretch limo to pick me up that day. I was uncomfortable with the entrance they made, but I appreciated their excitement for me.

My last prison stint was at Coldwater. All the prisoners who used to come hear me preach stood outside and began to sing "Hallelujah." I couldn't contain myself. The tears streamed down my face. I knew my work inside was done and that God was leading me to the next phase in my life.

The prisoners lined up, stood along the fence and continued to sing "Alleluia" while watching me walk out the doors. Going to prison is one thing, but to make a difference in the lives of others while you were there — that is something completely different. I thought about this as I took each step out. I understood that no one is worthy to be used by God. It is an honor to be that instrument.

When I walked down the halls of prison for the last time, I saw in

FINALLY, FREE

my mind the faces of the men who were healed there. David was healed from diabetes. He had it for nine years. Todd was healed from brittle bone disease and Mike from colitis. Of course, Daniel — the man who needed deliverance more than anyone I knew at the time — found Jesus.

My brothers, cousins and friends were with me on my drive home. I really didn't want them to pick me up like that, with such flash. I wanted to leave prison ready to live a simple life.

The drive from Coldwater to Southfield, Michigan, was filled with mixed emotions. I was happy to be going home, but sad to leave so many friends behind. I almost felt guilty for leaving. I asked everyone in the car how each was doing and about their families. They asked me questions, too. It was so good to be part of that group again.

It was raining that day. During the drive to my brother's home, I was anxious to hear about the others' lives. In prison, I was limited to 20 people I could call. There was excitement in the car. There was no talk about prison — just jubilation that I was out.

"You are going to be back on your feet," one of the guys said. "You are going to be fine."

I looked at them and smiled but was thinking how none of them really knew me and how my life was truly transformed. I wanted to tell them about God and how I was set free while still locked up, but I said nothing.

We arrived at my brother Kelly's house, and friends and relatives were there waiting to greet me. There were about 30 people waiting outside on the front lawn. Each one hugged me as I walked out of the car and toward the front door. The rain was now hitting hard. I looked at the raindrops and thought about how blessed I was at that moment.

There were more than 300 people inside the house. As time passed that night, I started to talk about God — that God was going to do mighty miracles and great things and people would see the manifestations of God's power.

I could see the strange looks on their faces. A few people laughed at my comments. One leaned over to my mother and tried to whisper, but I heard every word.

"Give him a few months," she said. "He will be back to normal."

The phone was ringing as I sat talking with different people. I took each phone call. I was talking to my other brothers, sisters, and friends around the country, and even to my ex-wife.

The excitement went on for days. People visited and called continuously as my sister-in-law and cousins cooked meals for all the visitors. People drifted in and out for weeks to see me. One summer years after I was released from prison, I bumped into the same cousins who snickered at me the night I talked about God at my brother's house on my first day home. I bumped into them while I was boating on a lake. "Hey, cousin!" one shouted at me. I looked over at the group on their boat.

"Hey guys," I said. "What's going on?"

"You proved us wrong, man. You did do what you said you were going to do. God is good."

Over the years, I met a few good priests in prison. Some from my own Chaldean community came to visit me. I began to think about those priests once I left prison. Of course, all those people who were the core volunteers for years in Lapeer — Mary, Michelle, Tom, Deacon Ed and his wife, Barbara — they built up my faith. Deacon Ed was instrumental in my journey. The elderly ladies, Estelle, and Carrie, whom I met in Lapeer, changed the course of my life and helped lead me to freedom.

My mom also had great faith that I would one day be set free. She prayed daily for me and never gave up. She relished in the relationship I had found in Christ. She anxiously waited for me to call when I was in prison. I am so grateful my mom saw me released from prison before she died. I would tell my mom the messages from the Lord, and she would get so excited.

When I went home, I felt this need deep inside my gut to preach. I knew that I was a preacher first. I loved talking to people about Jesus and the Scriptures. I felt this fire burning inside. Days upon returning home, I met with Bishop Ibrahim N. Ibrahim of the Chaldean Catholic Diocese in located in Southfield Michigan. The bishop told me to talk to the priests at the parishes.

One of my first stops was Mar Addai Church in Oak Park. Father Stephan Kallabat sat and prayed with me during that first meeting. I knelt and felt the Holy Spirit. Father Stephan could see that something was going on.

"What is it?" he asked.

"The Holy Spirit is here," I said.

"I know, son. I know," he said. "So, when do you want to start?"

"Whenever you are ready, Father."

"I am ready."

The following week, I started my speaking and healing ministry. On Jan. 9, 2006, I drove to Mar Addai Church for my first talk. The talks at the church lasted a year. They were scheduled every Thursday, and 80 to 100 people attended to hear me give my testimony and preach about Christ. I brought donuts and coffee to the talks. Then Father Andrew Younan from St. Joseph's Church in Troy Michigan heard about me.

"What's your story?" he asked me during a phone conversation one afternoon. "I want to meet with you."

"Okay, Father. Let's meet."

I went to his church on a Wednesday and sat down in his office.

"You got a half hour," he said. "Tell me everything you can about yourself."

"I can't cover my life in a half hour."

"Do your best. Tell me what you can."

I gave him the compact version of my testimony and as much as I could fit in about my life in prison the first 10 years, and what finally led me to my conversion and anointing. I was talking as fast as a nervous kid in the principal's office. After a half hour, Father Andrew looked at me with intensity.

"Okay, I heard enough. Let's go teach Bible study," he said. "You take the first half hour and I will take the second half hour."

"Okay. I am in."

We led the Bible study that night together and talked about building life on a solid foundation. "You have to know the depth," I told the crowd of nearly 100 people. "If you don't build your life on a solid foundation — on Christ — your life crumbles."

FINALLY, FREE

The greater the foundation, the more you know Jesus, and the greater the achievements. It is all through knowing Jesus. Father Andrew invited me to lead Bible study with him every week, and we did that for months until the young priest moved to California.

Later that year, I met a woman through a friend. She was talking nonsense, really. Her theology was wrong. I first recited Scripture and then I picked up the Bible and showed her. "Girl, you don't know what you are talking about," I told her.

"Yes, I do," she said.

"No, you don't know your theology."

I asked her about the church she attended and about Bible study. She attended a church my friend E.J. attended. I understood that her lack of understanding was not a reflection of the church, but her lack of seeking truth.

I started to attend the same Bible study and soon after asked E.J. if I could do the study with him. I opened it that year in September. I gave a talk at Drake Park in West Bloomfield for the end-of-summer picnic, which launched the next year's study. I saw Father Frank, who is now Bishop Francis, standing next to a car listening.

I preached about true faith that day, why Peter sank in the water and why, when you take your eyes off Jesus, you can't focus anymore. I spoke with great passion and conviction, often raising my voice. I almost shouted His Word.

I never knew Father Frank before that day. He ended up introducing me at opening day of Bible study. It was at St. Thomas Church, not far from the park. He introduced about five people before me and all of them had degrees. It was my turn and I stood up. "The

FREEDOM BEHIND BARS

only degree I have comes from Jackson Prison."

As I shared my story, I could hear the laughs and gasps. "But I got a treasure box and it is full of gems," I continued. "I want you to have some. I have emeralds, rubies and sapphires."

I kept thinking that all these people must think I was crazy, but I knew that if they got to know Jesus, they would get the treasure chest.

I continued Bible study at St. Thomas until the Eastern Catholic Re-Evangelization Center (ECRC) opened. E.J. introduced me to the co-founders of ECRC — Karam Bahnam and Neran Karmo— who, along with Father Frank, started this ministry.

I dreamt one night that Father Frank took a group of people to see the center, but I was standing in the middle of the ocean. The sun was beaming, and the water was crystal blue. I saw thousands of colored fish all around me. I knew God was telling me that He was going to use this center to bring all kinds of people to it. Sure enough, more than 500 people attend programs at the center each week. They have healing services, which I oversee today, and a variety of people of all walks of life attend. People from all nationalities — Italians, Albanians, Chaldeans, Pakistani and more — come to the healing services at ECRC. I have even had Muslims and atheists attend.

One evening, a group from ECRC was invited to a deacon's house in Southeast Michigan. His name was Bob, and he was a deacon through the Archdiocese of Detroit. He knew the Chaldean Diocese well. When the group arrived, I noticed one man in particular. I felt the Lord telling me something was wrong.

"Hey there, "I said to him. "How are you?"

"I am alright," he said. "I am good."

"No, you are not good. What is wrong with you?" I asked.

He looked at me with the familiar expression of "Who is this guy?" His lips began to quiver. He was now sitting on a swing. He began to cry.

"What's wrong, man?" I asked.

"I have cancer in my prostate," he said. "It was in remission and now it is back."

As soon as he uttered the words, I felt the flames of the Holy Spirit. The heat burst out from me like a flame thrower. I began to shout: "Don't you know that you are the servant of the Lord? Don't you know the devil is a liar? Get up. Let me pray on you in the name of Jesus."

The other guests heard me yelling. There were deacons everywhere, just looking at me. No one knew who I was, and I motioned for them to come over and lay hands on this man.

E.J.'s 6-year-old son laid his little hands over him, and we all prayed for him.

Six months later, I was invited to do a prayer service at Sacred Heart Major Seminary in Detroit. Dr. Peter Williamson asked me to pray with a large group of people that included seminarians, priests, and laypeople. It was nearing 2008. I asked Dr. Williamson about Deacon Bob, our friend. He told me that he was healed and that he was taking his wife on vacation. That is right. The guy was healed, and he went to Ireland on vacation. It was at that moment that we launched the ECRC healing ministry.

I would sometimes see Deacon Bob at the hospital praying with patients and bringing them the Eucharist.

FREEDOM BEHIND BARS

Prayers and healings continued

One day when praying at the seminary for the St. Paul Ministry, which is a group of people that started a charismatic movement. I totally felt Jesus take over. As soon as I started to thank the Lord for the day and for the ministry, I felt the Holy Spirit strike me like a lightning bolt on my back. I lit up. My face flushed red.

"Thank you, Jesus," I shouted. "I always know You are going to show up."

The second lightning bolt hit my back and again my body shined red. I felt the bolt going right through my body.

"Thank you, Lord," I prayed. "This is for Your glory."

For the third time the lightning bolt hit me.

"Jesus is in the house!" I shouted.

At that moment, I noticed a woman four or five rows back. I pointed to her and called her to the front.

"You, sitting in the back—come up here," I said. "Your back is going to be healed, once and for all."

People thought I knew her, but I had never met her before. She walked down to the front and began to cry while I began to shout.

"Jesus heal these bones!" I called out.

Another woman walked down and I spotted her. I never saw her again.

"You!" I shouted as I pointed at her. "Every day you ask for the gift from the Holy Spirit. Why don't you just believe Jesus will give it to you?"

"Oh my gosh; how did you know?"

"Stop saying and just believe it."

I then noticed a couple. They wanted to have a baby. I walked up to the woman and her husband and prayed on her.

"Receive the gift of life in the name of Jesus," I belted out. "Be consumed and have a baby."

She later did have a baby.

I then walked up to a teenager.

"You always ask Jesus to give you a double portion of Elijah," I said to her.

"Oh my gosh; I prayed that this morning," she said.

Elijah, a great prophet, was taken up and he held onto his mantel and said, "I won't let go until you give me a double portion of your spirit." He got the staph and mantel and the water of the Romans split.

There was another young woman with Multiple Sclerosis. I laid hands on her. She started burning with the Holy Spirit. She could not stop crying. So much heat emanated from her I thought I could fry eggs on her body. "Go back to your doctors and get a new diagnosis," I told her. Two years later, she was at St. Thomas waiting to see me. She couldn't wait to tell me she was MS free.

Dr. Williamson invited me to a non-denominational church in Jackson. There I started praying and doing healing prayers on people, and I was invited back several times.

My ministry started with non-Chaldeans. At one point, I was thinking of becoming a permanent deacon in the Latin Mass. It is hard for certain people to accept this gift, this healing ministry. I know it is not me. I cannot take credit. It is all for the glory of God.

"I don't heal," I tell people. "Jesus heals. The Holy Spirit comes through me. I have nothing to do with it. It is a gift. If people don't want me to use it on them, then I won't waste my time. They must answer to God. I do this only for Him."

This is God's gift and one I take very seriously. And through Jesus, the ministry "Jesus Light of Life" was born. This ministry is my vocation today.

Peter said in Acts 2:38, "Repent and be baptized and the gifts will be given to you and your family." In order to be healed, you have to repent from your sinful nature.

I wanted to be like Roger, who was a lifer in prison. He was the convert I talked about in the beginning. He was so devoted. I thought about Roger and his love for our Lord. I am so grateful that I, too, have that same love. The day I gave my life to Jesus will always be known as my rebirth. I was born that day as a true Christian. I was baptized as a baby, but reborn as an adult held behind bars.

I was sitting on a bunk when I dedicated my life to Jesus. It was 1999. "Lord, I give you my life," I said on that day. "I made a mess of things. I give you my life from here on out. I know you are going to do a better job than I did."

I didn't convert to my faith. I was already Catholic. It was a conversion of the heart. It was the first time I wanted a relationship with Christ. I understood for the first time that if you don't repent from the old ways and come into the new, God will never force

FINALLY, FREE

himself on you. Like He told me years earlier in a dream, *"I don't want people to come to be like a robot. If they renounce me, I will let them go."*

My ministry is about letting people know that God wants to get our attention again and again, but He will never force Himself on us. If you have repentance and baptism, a new beginning, you will find Jesus. If you make Jesus No. 1, he will make you No. 1.

The Miracle Prayer says it best. I recite this prayer before every healing service:

"Lord, Jesus, I come before You, just as I am. I am sorry for my sins, I repent of my sins, please forgive me. In Your name, I forgive all others for what they have done against me. I renounce Satan, the evil spirits and all their works. I give You my entire self. Lord Jesus, now and forever, I invite You into my life Jesus. I accept You as my Lord and Savior. Heal me, change me, strengthen me in body, soul and spirit. Come Lord Jesus, cover me with Your precious blood, and fill me with Your Holy Spirit, I love You Jesus. I praise You Jesus. I thank You Jesus. I shall follow You every day of my life.
Amen.

Mary my mother, Queen of Peace, St. Peregrine, the Cancer Saint, angels and Saints please help me. Amen."

"See, I am not that smart," I often explain to audiences. "It is all God."

I literally lamented over one verse in the Bible for three years. "For every branch that bears fruit must be pruned" (John 15:2).

FREEDOM BEHIND BARS

I didn't get it. If it was bearing fruit, why did it have to be pruned? God finally spoke to me: *"Because of the hardships of life"*

I finally understood. The hardship makes you stronger. It bears more fruit. It brings the best out of you. It is when you go through the hardships of life that your true faith comes out. You either fold or come closer to God. If you can get through the hardship, you will realize that God was always there to get you through it and you will bear more fruit than ever.

Job bores much through his pain and suffering, but God rewarded him mightily. God permitted the enemy to take everything from Job to test his faith and Job prevailed and God rewarded with twice as much. What should we take from this? Perseverance and faith produce great reward.

You'll also notice that God can turn evil into goodness (Romans 8:28 and Genesis 50:20).

Joseph was sold as a slave but became a governor. What you perceive to be evil, God turns into good. That is what God always does. It is not God who implements the evil. He permits the evil. He lets the devil have his way with us, only to lead us home to show us His infinite love beyond the world.

With addictions, when you go to Alcoholics Anonymous or other such groups, you have to first admit you need a higher power to help you. Surrendering is part of the 12 Steps. Even with divorce or other pains in this world, once you let your faith take over, you can overcome every obstacle. It is in total surrendering that you find true freedom.

If you want to surrender to the Lord, here are Scripture verses

FINALLY, FREE

to meditate on:

For I know well the plans I have in mind for you, says the LORD, plans for your welfare, not for woe! Plans to give you a future full of hope. When you call me, when you go to pray to me, I will listen to you. When you look for me, you will find me. Yes, when you seek me with all your heart (Jeremiah 29:11-13).

And hope does not disappoint, because the love of God has been poured out into our hearts through the Holy Spirit that has been given to us (Romans 5:5).

What then shall we say to this? If God is for us, who can be against us (Romans 8:31).

"Behold, I stand at the door and knock. If anyone hears my voice and opens the door, then I will enter his house and dine with him, and he with me (Revelation 3:20).

Chapter 10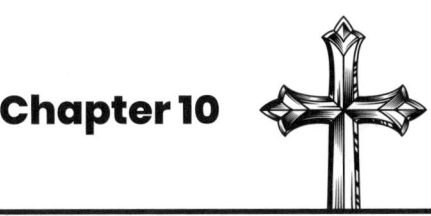

YOUR INDIVIDUAL CELL

"I sought the LORD, and he heard me, and delivered me from all my fears" -Psalm 34:4

✝

I stood in front of a crowd at an Eastern Catholic Re-Evangelization (ECRC) event talking about finding freedom while I shared my testimony.

"This is the thing," I told the audience. "It is in my own estimation that there are tens of thousands of people walking around this world free as a bird, as the old cliché goes, but they are locked up tighter than those on death row. They think they are free or appear to be free just because they are not living behind bars. In fact, they are not free. They are living in prison. It is the prison they created themselves or that society created, and they walked right into."

What is the name of your prison? Are you living on "addiction now?"

Millions of Americans are calling the prison of drugs and alcohol addiction their home.

According to a 2010 survey by the Closing the Addiction Treatment Gap (CATG) initiative, "Drug use is on the rise in this country and 23.5 million Americans are addicted to alcohol and drugs. That's approximately one in every 10 Americans older than the age of 12 — roughly equal to the entire population of Texas."

It's not the only addiction. There is sex addiction and those addicted to porn, like Officer Daniel.

I met two different men while working in my produce company, I owned from 2006 to 2015. I will first tell you about "Steve". He was married with kids. His wife was a faithful Catholic. He was a salesman. Every day he would show me pictures of women. I would sometimes walk in on him looking at porn on his computer. Every day I would tell him that porn was going to destroy him. I would talk to him about Jesus, and he would always reply, "Jesus wants us to be happy and sex makes me happy."

His wife caught him cheating on her by looking at his phone. She was devout in her faith. She was praying for him, and I was praying for them. At one point, his wife kicked him out of the house. He missed her and his family and wanted his life back. He finally gave his life to Jesus, and his wife forgave him. He never went back to porn again.

Unfortunately, I have met many others who have not been healed and who are still very much addicted to porn. Another man I met, also hooked on porn, was also married with kids. His addiction cost him his marriage. His wife did divorce him. "James" is still suffering. I see him occasionally and he has yet to give his life to Christ and find healing.

Gluttony is one of the seven deadly sins and there are food

YOUR INDIVIDUAL CELL

addicts all over the world — people who eat their pain away. There are shopping addicts who think they can buy their way out of their pain. Some people live in fear and anxiety every day. It's the No. 1 issue that comes up any time I am praying on someone.

I have many stories of people who have come to prayer service for healing from anxiety. I remember one young woman in her early 20s who came to service crying. She was dating a guy whom she loved. He strung her along, promising to marry her, but eventually left her. Her anxiety increased. She felt worthless. I prayed on her, and she fell out in the Spirit. The person is overcome by the Holy Spirit. They often feel heat sensation throughout the body, and their feet feel like cement, and they fall to the floor. The person becomes so heavy, and it is as if they feel glued to the floor. After that healing service, her anxiety began to subside.

Occasionally, she felt the anxiety coming back. This was the enemy getting back into her head. She would call me for prayer at all times of the day and night. I would pray with her. The anxiety continued to decrease. She continued to pray and give her life to Christ. She eventually met a new guy and got engaged.

Popular belief has it that the command "Do not be afraid" appears in some variation 365 times in the Bible: a daily reminder from God to live every day fearless. Some report the number of times is less than 365 but regardless of the exact number of times that fear is mentioned in the Bible, it's enough to know it is relevant; the reality is that the prison of fear is housing many of you.

Researchers have found that: (1)

- About 40 percent of the things, we worry about never happen;

- 30 percent of those things are in the past and can't be helped.
- 12 percent of our worries involve the affairs of others that are not even our business; and
- 10 percent relate to sickness, real or imagined.
- That means only 8 percent of the things we worry about are even likely to happen!

So, it has been said that worry is just interest paid on trouble before it happens and, in most cases, it never does. When you worry, there's a 92-percent chance you are focusing on something that will never be.

Fear and worry go hand in hand. They are BFFs, if you will. What did Jesus say about worry? Let's pick up the Bible and turn to the Gospel of Matthew:

"Therefore, I tell you, do not be anxious about your life, what you will eat or what you will drink, nor about your body, what you will put on. Is not life more than food and the body more than clothing? Look at the birds of the air: they neither sow nor reap nor gather into barns, and yet your heavenly Father feeds them. Are you not of more value than they? And which of you by being anxious can add a single hour to his span of life? And why are you anxious about clothing? Consider the lilies of the field, how they grow: they neither toil nor spin, yet I tell you, even Solomon in all his glory was not arrayed like one of these. But if God so clothes the grass of the field, which today is alive and tomorrow is thrown into the oven, will he not much more clothe you, O you of little faith? Therefore, do not be anxious, saying, 'What shall we eat?' or 'What shall we drink?' or 'What shall we wear?' For the Gentiles seek after all these things,

YOUR INDIVIDUAL CELL

and your heavenly Father knows that you need them all. But seek first the kingdom of God and his righteousness, and all these things will be added to you. Therefore, do not be anxious about tomorrow, for tomorrow will be anxious for itself. Sufficient for the day is its own trouble." (Matthew 6:25-34)

What prison are you living in? How will you be set free? Through Jesus Christ.

Some people might need medical help. There is great value in seeking help from a licensed therapist or psychiatrists. These professions exist for a reason, and I am neither. There are many well-trained experts in the field of addiction, but I encourage you to seek one out who is also Christ centered and with a strong Christian foundation.

Deliverance from evil is another part of a healing ministry but requires much more depth.

I am not going to get into the process of overcoming addiction from a medical perspective. I will leave that to the professionals. However, I can share with you some stories of healing I have witnessed in this ministry. Jesus Christ came to heal the sick. Go to Him.

There was one woman I met at healing service who could not forgive her sister for 27 years. She would not tell me why, but apparently it did bother her, and she cried uncontrollably. For 27 years she lost out on all that love and the bond between sisters, as well as with her nieces and nephews, because of her hostility. She missed all those holidays, birthdays, and everything because she could not forgive. She was more in prison than others actually behind bars. She knew it. She was trapped in hostility and couldn't get out. Her sister died before she ever made amends. I haven't spoken to her since that initial meeting, but I can only imagine her pain. Don't let that be you.

Release yourself from these prisons you have freely walked into. Jesus says, "If you don't forgive others, neither will your heavenly Father." (Matthew 6:14). Forgiveness heals us. It releases us from prison.

Here is an opportunity to do some introspection So, I ask again: What prison are you living in today? Are you living in fear and anxiety? Are you living in the prison of porn? Maybe you are living in resentment and hate. Get a journal and start writing about your prison and how it has affected your life. Then pick up the Bible and start meditating on Scripture that addresses your personal prison and how God shows us how to be released from our pain.

You may need professional help, and I urge you to seek it but do this along with your prayer and while focusing on Jesus. It is through Christ I found my freedom even while locked behind bars. I have prayed on and with thousands of people and have seen healing. God is good. He wants to heal you. He wants to free you. Go to Him and find your freedom.

Chapter 11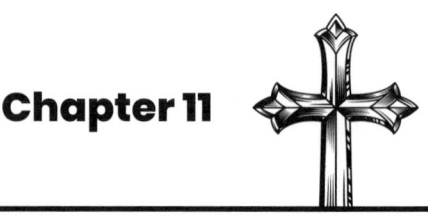

HEALED TO TELL

Seeing is believing, they say. Faith is blind. However, you don't have to take my word for any of this; maybe hearing or reading about those who have been healed by the Holy Spirit will help convince you of His power.

In this chapter, we share with you some of the many testimonials people have share with me over the years.

Blind Faith: Eyesight Miraculously Restored

George Washington Carver said, "Where there is no vision, there is no hope," but Ann Marie Di Legge's belief in healing went beyond sight.

Almost considered legally blind and to the point her doctor feared she may not be able to keep her driver's license, the 31-year-old at the time of her healing was boasting 20/30 vision.

Things began to change when the Italian American wife and mother of three met Adora Kassab Ibrahim, an old friend of her husband from school. They sat at the same table at a friend's wedding and began talking about faith. The two started praying for each other's families. Ibrahim mentioned the Eastern Catholic Re-Evangelization Center (ECRC), Tom Naemi's story and about healing mass.

Prayer and healing were not foreign to Di Legge. As a deep

HEALED TO TELL

believer, she grew up with her father praying in tongues and with a deep devotion to the Holy Spirit. He would pray over her while playing worship music and read the Bible over her at night. "I have had miracles happen to me," said Di Legge. "A pot of boiling oil spilled on my face at 3 years old and my father prayed over me. I have no scars from the injury."

Di Legge was born with a genetic eye disease called keratoconus, which is an abnormal cone-shaped protrusion of the cornea of the eye; she was told that she would eventually need cornea replacement. The surgery is done on one eye at a time and would require Di Legge to not drive for six months after each surgery, which would mean a year of not driving.

She had to wear two sets of contacts daily to be able to see.

As she grew older, her eyes became progressively worse, and eventually she developed an ulcer of the cornea. Doctors prescribed high doses of medicine and an anesthetic eye drop for the pain. "I felt like someone was cutting my eyes with glass," she said.

One night she fell asleep and woke up screaming from pain. Fluid oozed from her eye. "I told my husband this was it. My cornea was splitting, and I would go blind," she recalled.

She asked her husband to get holy water and the Bible, and to start praying over her by reading Scripture. She also woke up her 5-year-old daughter to pray over her. "She placed her hand over my eyes and began to speak another language," said Di Legge. "I asked her what she had said and she said, 'I asked Jesus to heal your eyes and He said yes.' My eyes stopped hurting and I went to bed.

"The next morning, I was going through my day and my eyes started pounding and became extremely sensitive to the light," she said. "I had a headache. I was looking for a priest to do healing. I knew I needed someone to pray over me. I made phone calls and could not find anyone and then remembered Adora mentioning Tom Naemi. I called him."

Tom was quite a distance away and was not able to see Di Legge. He told her that he would be free in a few days, but she could not wait. His healing mass was too far in the future. She was driving her car at the time and Naemi told her to pull over. He began to pray over her through the phone.

"He asked me first if I was a believer and if I believed in miracles," she remembered. "I said yes, of course. He told me to put my hands on my stomach. I felt heat and immediately I had no pain. I was crying and my head felt 10 times bigger than before. I started to blink my eyes and I was not feeling the same pain. When the heat went through me, my dogs ran from the back to the front of the car and began licking my face."

Believing she was healed, she called her husband and told him about Naemi's prayers. She went to the doctor the next morning. "He told me I still had scar tissue, but I was no longer in pain."

Di Legge still wanted more prayers and healing, so she planned to attend the healing mass at ECRC. She prepared by fasting for a week prior to the mass.

"On a Friday morning, Adora called me to tell me that day was the Feast of St. Lucia, the patron saint of eyes. I called my dad right after and said, 'I was born to be healed today.' He cried and laughed at the same time," she recalled.

She attended the healing mass and gave her testimony. This

HEALED TO TELL

time, Naemi prayed to her in person. She fell out by the Holy Spirit.

"The next morning, I woke up and saw a pair of eyes following me. There was not real color, but the eyes moved," she said. "I then blinked. I could not feel any callouses, and at first, I thought I fell asleep with my contacts on because I was able to see my husband sleeping next to me, which I would not be able to do without my contacts."

It was 4 a.m.

In amazement, Di Legge began walking around her house looking at things she could never see before, like images on the TV, and she didn't even have to feel her way through the house.

"I could see the fireplace, mantel, stockings … I could see the TV," she said with excitement. "I opened the Bible, and I could see words, and I wrote in my dream journal on the lines. I got on my knees and thanked the Lord. And the Christian channel was on and someone said there was going to be healing, and someone will experience partial healing and some will be restored. Some things were blurry. I said, 'Lord, in seven days, I am going to be restored.'"

She visited the doctor once again. For the first time in more than 10 years, she could see the large E on the eye chart. She returned seven days later and her vision was even stronger. She had 20/30 vision.

"God is amazing," she said. "My vision will be restored. I made a covenant with the Lord and I will not miss one Sunday mass. I am in awe of what He is surrounding me with right now. I am so grateful for Adora and Tom being in my life and for the Lord answering. It is a miracle. I am humbled He chose me to work through."

That was not the only miracle in her family. Days later, Tom visited Di Legge's grandmother, who hadn't walked in a year due to hip surgery. He prayed on her and she was able to stand up and walk to the bathroom.

"God is awesome, and He has been taking me on this journey," said DeLegge.

(Article originally appeared in The Chaldean News, January 2014)

Healed of Stage IV Cancer

It was Sept. 23, 2014, when Russell W. who was 59 years old learned about the healing mass at ECRC. When he came to healing mass, he was married for 36 years to his wife, Kathy. They have three children and four grandchildren. He was a practicing chiropractor in Portland for more than 32 years.

In early February 2014, he was diagnosed with urothelial carcinoma in his right kidney. He had surgery that April to remove the right kidney, right ureter, and right bladder cuff. The cancer had progressed to stage IV, was in the lymphatics around his aorta, and was inoperable. The medical oncologist prescribed very aggressive chemotherapy. He was scheduled to begin chemo on Monday, June 9.

Prior to that, a patient of his from St. Mary's Parish in Westphalia told a fellow parishioner, Connie, about a healing service and asked Connie to suggest it to him, since Connie had been one of Russell's lead employees for the last 12 years. Russell now encourages anyone who's aware of these healing services to tell everyone they know about it, because you never know whose life you'll change. After Connie told him and his wife about it, they decided to attend the service on Sunday, June 8 — one day before beginning chemo. "That day changed everything for me," said Russell.

"As Father Mathias started to speak about preparing yourself, he said we had to forgive anyone we were harboring ill will toward for whatever they had done against us," said Russell. "I couldn't believe how freeing that was. He said some people may experience a warm feeling or tingling as they prepare to come forward. I had come to ask God to heal me of cancer."

Russell wanted to spend more time on Earth, grow old with his wife and watch his grandkids grow up. He made a covenant with God deep down in his heart to do whatever He asked if God would show mercy on him and allow him to recover. This was totally different from the "deals of the head" we make with God. "If you'll just clear my child's fever, God, I'll thank you every day forever." But when the fever is gone, so is the promise to God. "If I just get a good grade on this hard exam, I'll praise you every day." But when the test is passed, so is the daily praise. Deals of the head. He made a covenant "of the heart."

"God rewards us when we come to Him sincerely and turn to him asking for his help," said Russell. "He had no reason, I thought, to answer my prayer. I hadn't practiced my faith in years; I didn't pray regularly and had grown far from living in His presence or following His commandments.

"Before the alter call, I began to perspire, uncontrollable perspiration. I had a oneness of purpose to get to the altar and be prayed on. By the time I got to Tom Naemi, I was soaked to the skin from perspiration. He asked me why I was there, and I told him to ask to be healed from kidney cancer. He put his hands on me and began to pray. I went down. I couldn't open my eyes or move my body. He called four others to put their hands on me and pray. I could hear them all and feel them all but couldn't move. Once they left, I just laid there. I don't know how long I laid there."

While out in the Spirit, God told Russell very clearly that he would recover from cancer, but not without pain and not without consequence for how far he had grown away from Him and the extent to which God had to go to get his attention. Russell continued to share what he experienced.

"Shortly thereafter, I decided to get up but when I went to move, I still couldn't open my eyes or move my body. I then realized my legs were straight, stiff and trembling. I had seen others before me lying on the floor trembling and now I knew why. So, I rested until the spasms and trembling stopped. I decided a second time to get up, and my eyes opened, and my legs relaxed, and I was able to stand. I was very disoriented and crying. I looked for Kathy but couldn't find her. She was farther down the line on the floor."

Russell realized he was in the way and went to return to his pew. He walked to the back of the church. His friends and family members were there who he walked right past on his way to get in line and never saw. "I was still crying as I tried to explain what just happened," he noted. "I couldn't explain what just happened. I couldn't explain it or discuss it without crying for a few weeks. When we left, Kathy and I talked all the way to Ann Arbor."

She had told Tom that she was there for relief of her arthritis so she could help her husband in his battle with cancer. Tom asked if she meant 'that guy down there,' pointing to me. She said yes and he said, 'That guy's on fire.' I told Kathy what God told me when I was on the floor. I told her I was going to recover, that I would be okay. She asked me if I was going to do the chemo. I said, 'Yes, I am supposed to. I was told I was going to be healed and survive, but that it would not be without pain or without consequence for how far I had grown from God and to what lengths He had to go to get my attention.'"

The next morning, Russell started a very aggressive chemo plan. He had chemo with two drugs on Monday. On Tuesday, he had seven hours of chemo with three drugs. Monday night, in bed in Ann Arbor, he was startled awake by a grotesque dark figure right in his face. It was head and shoulders and neck. He bolted upright in bed in the dark, but it was still there. He pushed it away with his hands. He laid back down, breathing hard, trying to figure out what just happened. It reappeared just as clear and just as close. He sat up and pushed it away again. The third time, he pushed and yelled, "GET OUT OF HERE!" It never returned. Russell believes he faced the devil and cast him away.

Within days, the nausea was unbelievable, and the constipation was worse. He was miserable, but he realized that he wasn't afraid. He hasn't been afraid since he received the Holy Spirit. He had begun praying daily and reading devotionals daily. Constipation nearly hospitalized him. A few weeks into treatment, he developed sores in his mouth that were extremely painful and made eating very difficult. His immune system bottomed out during weeks two and three. "Pain and consequences, but I'll be okay," he thought.

He was praying multiple times daily and reading the Bible. He was raised Catholic and had said the Rosary thousands of times, but, for the first time in his life, he was praying it — thoughtfully praying it with conviction.

"The words I had spoken thousands of times had whole new meaning," he said. "I can hardly get through the Sorrowful Mysteries without crying when I realize what Jesus suffered for us. The 'Our Father' is completely different when you live by 'Thy will be done on

Earth' and '… as we forgive those who trespass against us.' I always used to emphasize 'Give us this day our daily bread' and 'forgive us our trespasses,' asking for mine but not willing to carry the other side of the prayer. 'And lead us not into temptation but deliver us from evil' can be said any time, all day long, to stay in the presence of God as He tells us what to do.

"The same Scriptures I've heard all my life have new meaning to me now. I understand Jesus's parables. I see all of the Bible's relevance to today, to my life. I see that Jesus's words save us. The immeasurable magnitude of God's love for us. The road to a full life with peace and joy, Him keeping his promises to us if we just keep ours to Him. As I said before, I have no fear. Imagine being able to face life-threatening cancer without fear. It aids your recovery, I'll tell you. The symptoms I was supposed to have — severe nausea, constipation, mouth sores, a metallic taste to all of my food, difficulty eating — I've had nothing since the first cycle. By the end of cycle 3, the CT scan showed cancer around/in my lymphatics around my aorta was gone."

The doctor was elated and kept going on and on about how lucky they were the treatment was so effective. He was surprised by Russell's calmness, unexcited demeanor and kept repeating how great it was. He didn't realize that by the time of that test, Russell had known it was gone for three months and had been thanking God for that every day.

"I strive now to stay in His presence all day, every day," said Russell. "I speak out His name for support all day just to bring my awareness back to HIM. For that, He offers us love, support and forgiveness beyond our comprehension. He gives us the gift of another day on Earth with our loved ones."

HEALED TO TELL

How are you going to use that gift today? How are you going to prepare to use that gift again tomorrow? "Don't waste those gifts, these days," said Russell. "Praise Him and thank Him every day. Bring your wants and needs to Him every day and He'll sort them through with you and guide your choices that day. Live without fear. Live in His light without darkness."

Russell knew not only was his life saved but so was his eternity. "I went that day for physical healing. What I received was definitely a two-for-one; I also received spiritual healing."

Russell went to a second healing service at Flint Holy Redeemer. He went to thank God for the healing of his body and the time He's giving him on Earth. He went to thank Him for his eternity. But he also went to act as a surrogate for the granddaughter of one of his best friends. "Katie was stricken with non-Hodgkin's lymphoma at age 17," said Russell. "She is a great Christian girl with good morals, standards, and work ethic, but not someone who had yet received the Holy Spirit. He went and asked God to heal her of her cancer and fill her with the Holy Spirit for the good she would do on this Earth in His name."

Russell explained it to Father Mathias and again was overcome with the Holy Spirit. As he and the others prayed over him for Katie, he again could hear their words and feel their touch, but not open his eyes or move his body. He was aware of his stiff legs and the trembling and that he was crying, but he again couldn't open his eyes or move. As time passed, he could open his eyes, but still not move. He just laid there until the Spirit settled in him and then he was able to move and get up.

"I feel very strongly that the Holy Spirit came to Katie," he said. "She is just now beginning to come to grips with what all that

FREEDOM BEHIND BARS

means — the place of conceding to 'Thy will be done on Earth as it is in Heaven.' Her grandparents, who have received Jesus, are guiding her to understanding and accepting that giant, eternity changing step of 'letting go and letting God.' Stepping out of the way to allow His will to be done in you, through you — whatever He calls us to do. I continue to pray for her fully giving herself to God so she can know the peace of being safely and eternally in His hands."

Healing from a Neck Growth

In March of 2009, Keith D. noticed a small growth on his neck. Initially, he thought it was a pimple and that it would go away. When it grew and began looking ugly, his wife encouraged him to have his doctor look at it. He said that it appeared to be a keratoacanthoma growth. In most cases, keratoacanthoma grows rapidly, is benign, and disappears within six months, usually leaving a scar. He said that in some cases, however, this type of growth is cancerous (squamous cell carcinoma) and should be quickly dealt with. He ordered a biopsy to be taken a few weeks later. Keith subsequently saw his chiropractor for something unrelated and she advised against the biopsy in favor of homeopathic treatment of oil of oregano (a natural antiseptic) applied directly to the growth.

"I was a bit torn about what to do, but prayerfully canceled the biopsy appointment," he said. "I had to cover the growth with a bandage so others wouldn't have to look at it. My wife was still concerned about cancer, so I was happy to hear that Tom Naemi was coming to our prayer meeting to pray with people for healing."

Keith received prayer and felt the presence of the Lord immediately. As Tom prayed, he said, "You don't have cancer." He continued to pray and said something to the effect that the growth would

HEALED TO TELL

be gone within a week. "I felt a lot better about the situation and continued with my treatment," said Keith. "The growth appeared to be shriveling up and within four days it dropped off. There appears to be no scar. I believe that I am healed. Praise the Lord!"

ABOUT THE AUTHOR

Tom Naemi is an international speaker; he has given his testimony and has spoken to thousands of people around the globe. Tom has participated in Prison Ministries since his release from prison in 2005. He is an active member of Eastern Catholic Re-evangelization Center (ECRC) where he oversees the monthly healing mass. He also conducts a bible study group with EJ Jonna. He has a YouTube Series produced by ECRC's Mar Toma Productions called Freedom Behind Bars. The series has aired on the Noursat Network around the globe.

Vanessa Denha Garmo is a Communications Strategist, Evangelist, Speaker, Christian Life and, Leadership and Career Coach, Content Creator and host of Epiphany on Ave Maria Radio. She has a master's degree in Communications from Spring Arbor University and is working on a second Master's in Catechetics and Evangelization from Franciscan University Steubenville. She is the founder of Epiphany Communications & Coaching. Vanessa also hosts the weekly Public Affairs show It's Your Community heard on WJR AM 760, 96.3 FM and 93.1 FM. She is married with a daughter.

ADVANCE PRAISE

Tom Naemi is the real thing, a living miracle of the kind that only Jesus Christ can accomplish. This book bears witness to the amazing transformation that the Holy Spirit can bring about in a man—from violence and hatred to love and healing compassion. In Tom's case, the Lord chose a criminal and prisoner, set him free, and empowered him with healing and evangelization gifts to serve others. The healing stories are wonderful! We have a great God!

– Dr. Peter S. Williamson, Adam Cardinal Maida Chair of Sacred Scripture

Sacred Heart Major Seminary

Tom Naemi's testimony is extraordinary! The riveting stories of his own conversion and of the miracles God worked through him in prison will convince readers that truly nothing is impossible with God. This book will give hope to those who think they can never be freed from the prisons of anger, revenge, addiction, anxiety, and fear. I look forward to giving away many copies.

– Dr. Mary Healy, professor of Scripture at Sacred Heart Major Seminary

"Tom tells it like it is and has expressed well what it's like on both sides of the prison bars. Being locked up, away from family and friends is one Hell, but existing with some of the inmates for an extended time is a worse Hell on earth. When I was 'locked up' and exposed to prison life one evening a week for 25 years, I always thanked God that I was in prison as a visitor. And like Tom, I was blessed to be called by Jesus to be an instrument to bring Him to the inmates. My reward was having inmates giving me heartfelt thanks. I received many notes over the years including from one person who said, "I owe my life to God the Father and for using you as a tool to change my life, I am eternally thankful". He was baptized a month later. I'm sure that Tom has, and will continue to hear, similar expressions of thanks for his prison ministry and for sharing his story"

-Ron Reynolds, in Prison Ministry for 25 Years.